Mezzos and contraltos

Baker Klose Ferrier Simionato Höngen

with valuable assistance from Malcolm Walker

Discographies compiled by John Hunt

mezzos and contraltos

- 3 Acknowledgement
- 4 Introduction
- 7 Dame Janet Baker
- 99 Margarete Klose
- 129 Kathleen Ferrier
- 173 Giulietta Simionato
- 215 Elisabeth Höngen
- 243 Credits

Mezzo and Contraltos
Published by John Hunt.
Designed by Richard Chluparty
© 1998 John Hunt
reprinted 2009
ISBN 978-1-901395-96-9

Sole distributors:
Travis & Emery,
17 Cecil Court,
London, WC2N 4EZ,
United Kingdom.
(+44) 20 7 459 2129.
sales@travis-and-emery.com

acknowledgement: these publications have been made possible by contributions
and advance subscriptions from

Masakasu Abe, Chiba
Richard Ames, New Barnet
Stefano Angeloni, Frasso Sabino
Stathis Arfanis, Athens
Yoshihiro Asada, Osaka
Jack Atkinson, Tasmania
Brian Capon, Glasgow
Eduardo Chibas, Caracas
Robert Christoforides, Fordingbridge
F. De Vilder, Bussum
Richard Dennis, Greenhithe
John Derry, Newcastle-upon-Tyne
Hans-Peter Ebner, Milan
Henry Fogel, Chicago
Peter Fu, Hong Kong
Nobuo Fukumoto, Hamamatsu
Peter Fulop, Toronto
James Giles, Sidcup
Guy Glenet, Bordeaux
Jens Golumbus, Hamburg
Jean-Pierre Goossens, Luxembourg
Johann Gratz, Vienna
Michael Harris, London
Tadashi Hasegawa, Nagoya
Naoya Hirabayashi, Tokyo
Martin Holland, Sale
Bodo Igesz, New York
Richard Igler, Vienna
Shiro Kawai, Tokyo

Andrew Keener, New Malden
Koji Kinoshita, Osaka
Detlef Kissmann, Solingen
John Larsen, Mariager
Elisabeth Legge-Schwarzkopf DBE, Zürich
John Mallinson, Hurst Green
Carlo Marinelli, Rome
Finn Moeller Larsen, Virum
Philip Moores, Stafford
Bruce Morrison, Gillingham
W. Moyle, Ombersley
Alan Newcombe, Hamburg
Hugh Palmer, Chelmsford
Jim Parsons, Sutton Coldfield
Laurence Pateman, London
James Pearson, Vienna
Johann Christian Petersen, Hamburg
Tully Potter, Billericay
Patrick Russell, Calstock
Yves Saillard, Mollie-Margot
Neville Sumpter, Northolt
Yoshihiko Suzuki, Tokyo
H.A. Van Dijk, Apeldoorn
Mario Vicentini, Cassano Magnago
Hiromitsu Wada, Chiba
Urs Weber, St Gallen
Nigel Wood, London
G. Wright, Romford
Ken Wyman, Brentwood

mezzos and contraltos

Like its male counterparts in the baritone and bass departments, the female voice at the lower ends of the range can encompass a number of differing voice types. The high mezzo can venture fearlessly into soprano range (particularly useful for the song and bel canto recitalist in repertoire from Handel to Donizetti). Dramatic (operatic) mezzo voices can command a range of stage roles, many of them so-called trouser roles, drawn from the German, Italian and French repertory (Fricka, Waltraute, Ortrud, Amme, Lady Macbeth, Eboli, Amneris, Orfeo, Dorabella, Cherubino, Carmen, Dalila). The genuine contralto finds a true home in the worlds of Lieder and the oratorios of Handel, Mendelssohn and Elgar.

As usual when one takes a selection of voices from such a category, one encounters those who embrace a wide variety of work both from the concert and operatic fields (true here in the cases of the Germans Margarete Klose and Elisabeth Höngen). Then there are those who remain very much within their native linguistic framework (Giulietta Simionato), or who feel most at home in the concert hall (Kathleen Ferrier - but who can say that this emphasis may not have changed had the singer's very early death not intervened?). Finally, in Dame Janet Baker, we have an example of the singer who fulfils a lifetime of activity with the resolute emphasis of taking on only work with which she feels a committed temperamental affinity.

As far as the discographical results of Baker's career are concerned, they present us with a particularly intriguing and far-ranging body of recordings, which will serve as models of their kind for future generations. In the field of opera the aficianados may have this or that regret that she did not venture further afield, or at least did not bring to the recording studio her peerless interpretations of the Strauss roles Oktavian and Komponist. Conductor Otto Klemperer is supposed to have envisaged her for the part of Fricka in a complete recording of "Die Walküre" which ultimately did not materialise.

Perhaps hectoring, let alone villainy, was not in Janet Baker's vocal armoury, whereas it lay at the very centre of those operatic figures who were the mainstay of the careers of Margarete Klose and Elisabeth Höngen. Broadly speaking, Höngen was based in Dresden and (following conductor Karl Böhm) Vienna, Klose in Berlin. Both lent their names to many an important operatic revival, and both featured on many landmark recordings until well into the 1950s, that first great period of complete opera recordings for the new long-playing format. Klose is heard as Ortrud in recordings of Wagner's "Lohengrin" conducted by both Kempe and Schüchter, and as Fricka for Wilhelm Furtwängler. Höngen ranges from Carmen and Lady Macbeth to the Amme in Decca's pioneering "Frau ohne Schatten" recording of 1955, and on to the Witch in "Hänsel und Gretel" as late as 1964.

At the time of her heyday, Giulietta Simionato was one of a group of Italian operatic mezzos (Stignani, Barbieri, Cossotto were others) whose vocal and declamatory ease has made later generations seem less well-schooled and less full-blooded.

Again, Simionato became virtually a household name for LP recordings of the standard Italian repertory. I discovered in the course of preparing her discography that she had seriously considered taking on the ultimate vocal challenge of Bellini's Norma! And in passing, I am indebted to a recent publication by Baskerville Publishers Inc. (Simionato: How Cinderella became Queen): this lists many recorded live performances of the mezzo which it suggests have been issued in Italy, but as I can find no evidence of publication I have listed them as unpublished.

Kathleen Ferrier's status as one of the 20th century's great voices rests on a performance legacy of less than 10 years' work, the recorded evidence coming from an even shorter time-span. The remarkable ease of projection and the warm velvet-like tone certainly recall Kirsten Flagstad, whose career was coming to its natural close just as Ferrier's was being sadly forced to end. However, the appeal of Ferrier's directly produced and emotionally honest voice (there was no trace of sophistication or affectation) gave her the status of a national institution which was accessible far beyond the confines of mere classical music enthusiasts.

The discographies are arranged chronologically by composer and set out in 3 columns: the first one gives place and date of the recording, the second one other participating principal soloists, orchestra and conductor (if only one name appears, it can in the majority of cases be assumed that this is an accompanying pianist). The third column gives catalogue issue numbers (first issues and subsequent editions in the most important territories in the formats of 78, 45, LP and CD).

In the case of complete opera recordings, the second column of the discography is headed by an indication of which role the artist takes in that opera; excerpts from a major work are of course only listed if they feature the artist whose discography is being covered.

Abbreviations for orchestras in this volume are the familiar ones for London, Vienna and Berlin orchestras (LPO, LSO, BPO, VPO, VSO) with the addition of ASMIF for Academy of St.Martin-in-the-Fields.

For German Lieder recordings, the first line of the set text is given in brackets where this differs from the song's actual title, or alternatively an indication is given when a song is drawn from a larger work or cycle (for example, Der Lindenbaum/Die Winterreise).

I am always glad to hear from readers who can furnish additional information on any recording, as there are bound to be instances where the data I have assembled is incomplete.

Dame Janet Baker
born 1933

THOMAS ARNE (1710-1778)

where the bee sucks

London	Instrumentalists	LP: EMI HQS 1091/ESD 100 6421
9-10		LP: Angel 36456
February		
1967		

10 Baker

JOHANN SEBASTIAN BACH (1685-1750)

matthäus-passion

Munich June- August 1979	Mathis, Schreier, Fischer-Dieskau, Salminen Munich Bach Orchestra & Chorus K.Richter	LP: DG 2712 005/2723 067 CD: DG 413 6132/427 7042

Although original documentation indicated that Baker took a minor part in Klemperer's 1962 Columbia recording of the Matthäus-Passion, the artist herself confirms that this was not the case

johannes-passion, excerpt (es ist vollbracht)

London 1979	ASMIF Marriner	LP: EMI ASD 3265/1C063 02785

mass in b minor

London
18 October-
10 November
1967
	Giebel, Gedda,
	Prey, Crass
	BBC Chorus
	New Philharmonia
	Klemperer
		LP: EMI AN 195-197/SAN 195-197/SLS 930/
		   SMA 91691-91693/1C165 00090-00092/
		   1C197 54135-54145
		LP: Angel 3730
		CD: EMI CMS 763 3642
		Excerpts
		LP: EMI HQS 1407
		LP: Angel 4515

London 16 November 1967	Giebel, Gedda, Prey, Crass BBC Chorus New Philharmonia Klemperer	CD: Arkadia CD 727/CDGI 727
London 28 June- 10 July 1977	Marshall, Tear, Ramey ASMIF and Choir Marriner	LP: Philips 6769 002 CD: Philips 416 4152 Excerpts LP: Philips 6527 099

magnificat

London	Popp, Pashley,	LP: EMI ASD 2533/1C063 01991
8-11	Tear, Hemsley	LP: Angel 36615
May	New Philharmonia	CD: EMI CDM 764 6342
1968	Orchestra & Chorus	
	Barenboim	

magnificat, excerpt (et exsultavit)

London	ASMIF	LP: EMI ASD 3265/1C063 02785
1979	Marriner	

weihnachts-oratorium

London	Ameling, Tear,	LP: EMI SLS 5098/1C153 02890-82892
August	Fischer-Dieskau	CD: EMI CZS 569 5032
1976	Kings College	
	Choir	
	ASMIF	
	Marriner	

weihnachts-oratorium, excerpt (schlafe mein liebster!)

London	ASMIF	LP: EMI ASD 3265/1C063 02785/SLS 5275
1979	Marriner	

cantata no 6, excerpt (hoch gelobter gottessohn)

London	ASMIF	LP: EMI ASD 3265/1C063 02785
1979	Marriner	

cantata no 11, excerpt (bleibe doch, mein liebstes leben)

London	ASMIF	LP: EMI ASD 3265/1C063 02785
1979	Marriner	

cantata no 34, excerpt (wohl euch, ihr auserwählten seelen)

London	ASMIF	LP: EMI ASD 3265/1C063 02785
1979	Marriner	

12 Baker

cantata no 79 "gott der herr ist sonn' und schild"

Stuttgart July 1967	Ameling, Altmeyer, Sotin South German Madrigalchor Consortium clasicum Gönnenwein	LP: EMI ASD 2396/1C063 29017

cantata no 80 "ein' feste burg ist unser gott"

Stuttgart July 1967	Ameling, Altmeyer, Sotin South German Madrigalchor Consortium classicum Gönnenwein	LP: EMI ASD 2381/1C063 29017 LP: Angel 36419 CD: EMI CZS 568 6702/CZS 568 7522

cantata no 82 "ich habe genug"

London July 1966	Bath Festival Orchestra Menuhin	LP: EMI ALP 2302/ASD 2302/SEOM 8/ SXLP 30289/1C053 00318/SLS 5275 LP: Angel 36419 CD: EMI CZS 568 7522

cantata no 129, excerpt (gelobt sei der herr mein gott!)

London 1979	ASMIF Marriner	LP: EMI ASD 3265/1C063 02785

cantata no 147 "herz und mund und tat und leben"

London July 1970	Ameling, Partridge, Shirley-Quirk Kings College Choir ASMIF Willcocks	LP: EMI HQS 1254/1C063 02230

cantata no 148 "bringet dem herrn ehre!"

Stuttgart	Ameling, Altmeyer,	LP: EMI ASD 2396/1C063 29012
July	Sotin	
1967	South German	
	Madrigalchor	
	Consortium classicum	
	Gönnenwein	

cantata no 149 "man singet mit freuden von sieg"

Stuttgart	Ameling, Altmeyer,	LP: EMI ASD 2396/1C063 28490
July	Sotin	
1967	South German	
	Madrigalchor	
	Consortium classicum	
	Gönnenwein	

cantata no 159 "sehet, wir geh'n hinauf gen jerusalem"

London	Tear,	LP: Decca OL 295/SOL 295
February	Shirley-Quirk	CD: Decca 430 2602
1966	St Anthony	
	Singers	
	ASMIF	
	Marriner	

cantata no 161, excerpt (komm du süsse todesstunde!)

London	ASMIF	LP: EMI ASD 3265/1C063 02785
1979	Marriner	

14 Baker

cantata no 169 "gott soll mein herze haben"

London July 1966	Ambrosian Singers Bath Festival Orchestra Menuhin	LP: EMI ALP 2302/ASD 2302/SXLP 30289/ 1C053 00318 LP: Angel 36419

cantata no 170 "vergnügte ruh, beliebte seelenlust"

London February 1966	ASMIF Marriner	LP: Decca OL 295/SOL 295 CD: Decca 430 2602 <u>Excerpts</u> LP: Decca GRV 5 CD: Decca 440 4132

cantata no 190, excerpt (lobe, zion, deinen gott!)

London 1979	ASMIF Marriner	LP: EMI ASD 3265/1C065 02785

bist du bei mir/geistliche lieder und arien

London 1979	ASMIF Marriner	LP: EMI ASD 3265/1C063 02785

ave maria, arranged by gounod

Cambridge 30-31 October 1980	Ledger	LP: EMI ASD 3981

MISTER BARRINGCLOE (17th century)

jehovah reigns!

Snape 14 June 1971	Leppard, Hall	CD: BBC Music Magazine MM 143

LUDWIG VAN BEETHOVEN (1770-1827)

missa solemnis

London 1-10 May 1975	Harper, Tear, Sotin New Philharmonia Chorus LPO Giulini	LP: EMI SLS 989/1C163 02740-02741 LP: Angel 3836 CD: EMI CMS 565 8272/CZS 569 4402/ CZS 762 6932

mass in c

London 15-18 September 1970	Ameling, Altmeyer, Rintzler New Philharmonia Orchestra & Chorus Giulini	LP: EMI ASD 2661/1C063 02124 LP: Angel 36775 CD: EMI CMS 566 3292

scottish folksong settings: polly stewart; the sweetest lad was jamie; faithfu' johnie; cease your funning; bonny laddie

London 1975	G.Malcolm, Menuhin, Pople	LP: EMI ASD 3167/1C063 02709 <u>Bonny laddie</u> LP: EMI SLS 5275

freudvoll und leidvoll/egmont

London 1973	ECO Leppard	LP: Philips 9500 307/6767 001

ah perfido!; no non turbati!, concert arias

London 1973	ECO Leppard	LP: Philips 9500 307/6767 001

VINCENZO BELLINI (1801-1835)

i capuleti ed i montecchi

London 16-26 June 1975	Role of Romeo Sills, Gedda, Lloyd, Herincx Alldis Choir New Philharmonia Patanè	LP: EMI SLS 986/1C193 02713-02715

HECTOR BERLIOZ (1803-1869)

béatrice et bénédict

London 19-22 December 1977	Role of Béatrice Eda-Pierre, Watts, Tear, Lloyd, Bastin, Allen, Van Allan Alldis Choir LSO Davis	LP: Philips 6700 121/6707 019 CD: Philips 416 9522/456 3872

les troyens, act 5 scenes 2 and 3

Watford 14-15 September 1969	Role of Dido Greevy, Erwen, Howell Ambrosian Singers LSO Gibson	LP: EMI ASD 2516/1C063 02426 LP: Angel 36695 CD: EMI CDM 769 5442 Excerpts LP: EMI SEOM 8/SLS 5275

la damnation de faust

Paris September- October 1969	Gedda, Bacquier, Thau Paris Opéra Chorus Orchestre de Paris Prêtre	LP: EMI SLS 947/1C165 02019-02020 LP: Angel 3758 CD: EMI CZS 568 5832 Excerpts LP: EMI SLS 5275

la mort de cléopatre

Watford 14-15 September 1969	LSO Gibson	LP: EMI ASD 2516/1C063 02426 LP: Angel 36695 CD: EMI CDM 769 5442/CZS 568 5832
London 6-10 March 1979	LSO Davis	LP: Philips 9500 683 CD: Philips 416 9602

18 Baker

herminie, scena

London 6-10 March 1979	LSO Davis	LP: Philips 9500 683 CD: Philips 416 9602

l'enfance du christ

Watford 24-27 October 1976	Tappy, Allen, Rouleau, Bastin Alldis Choir LSO Davis	LP: Philips 6700 106/6768 002 CD: Philips 416 9492

les nuits d'été

London 22-23 August 1967	New Philharmonia Barbirolli	LP: EMI ASD 2444/1C063 01867/1C065 02122/ SLS 5013 LP: Angel 36505 CD: EMI CDM 769 5442 Excerpts LP: EMI SEOM 8/SLS 5275
London January 1990	City of London Sinfonia Hickox	CD: Virgin CUV 61118/VBD 561 4692

la belle voyageuse; la captive; zaide

London January 1990	City of London Sinfonia Hickox	CD: Virgin CUV 61118/VDB 561 4692

GIOVANNI BONONCINI (1670-1747)

deh più a me non v'ascendete

London January 1978	ASMIF Marriner	LP: Philips 9500 557 CD: Philips 434 1732

WILLIAM BOYCE (1711-1779)

tell me, lovely shepherd!

London 9-10 February 1967	Moore	LP: EMI HQS 1091/ESD 100 6421 LP: Angel 36456

MAY BRAHE (1885-1956)

bless this house

Cambridge 30-31 October 1980	Ledger	LP: EMI ASD 3981

20 Baker

JOHANNES BRAHMS (1833-1897)

alto rhapsody

London
15 December
1970
	Alldis Choir
	LPO
	Boult
		LP: EMI ASD 2746/ASD 3260/SLS 5275/
		    SLS 5009/SXLP 30259/1C053 02179/
		    1C065 02758
		LP: Angel 37199
		CD: EMI CDC 747 8542/CDM 568 0142/
		    CDM 769 4242/CZS 568 6552

London February 1989	LSO Chorus City of London Sinfonia Hickox	CD: Virgin CUV 56589/VBD 561 4692

4 ernste gesänge

London October- November 1977	Previn	LP: EMI ASD 3605/1C065 03279 CD: EMI CZS 568 6672

lieder with viola obbligato: gestillte sehnsucht; geistliches wiegenlied

London October- November 1977	Previn, Aronowitz	LP: EMI ASD 3605/1C065 03279 CD: EMI CZS 568 6672

duets: die nonne und der ritter; vor der tür; es rauschet das wasser; der jäger und sein liebchen

London 21-23 August 1969	Fischer-Dieskau Barenboim	LP: EMI ASD 2553/1C063 02041 CD: EMI CZS 568 6672 <u>Es rauschet das Wasser</u> LP: EMI EX 29 04293

auf dem kirchhofe (der tag ging regenschwer und sturmbewegt)

London October- November 1977	Previn	LP: EMI ASD 3605/1C065 03279

der jäger (mein lieb ist ein jäger)

London October- November 1977	Previn	LP: EMI ASD 3605/1C065 03279

das mädchen spricht (schwalbe, sag mir an!)

London 1965	Isepp	LP: Saga XID 5277/STXID 5277 CD: Saga SCD 9001

die mainacht (wann der silberne mond durch die gesträuche blinkt)

London 1965	Isepp	LP: Saga XID 5277/STXID 5277 CD: Saga SCD 9001

nachklang (regentropfen aus den bäumen)

London October- November 1977	Previn	LP: EMI ASD 3605/1C065 03279

nachtigall (o nachtigall, dein süsser schall!)

London 1965	Isepp	LP: Saga XID 5277/STXID 5277 CD: Saga SCD 9001

22 Baker

sapphische ode (rosen brach ich)

London   Previn   LP: EMI ASD 3605/1C065 03279
October-
November
1977

ständchen (der mond steht über dem berge)

London   Previn   LP: EMI ASD 3605/1C065 03279
October-
November
1977

therese (du milchjunger knabe)

London   Previn   LP: EMI ASD 3605/1C065 03279
October-
November
1977

vergebliches ständchen (guten abend, mein schatz)

London   Previn   LP: EMI ASD 3605/1C065 03279
October-
November
1977

von ewiger liebe (dunkel, wie dunkel, in wald und in flur)

London   Isepp   LP: Saga XID 5277/STXID 5277
1965   CD: Saga SCD 9001

wie melodien zieht es mir

London   Previn   LP: EMI ASD 3605/1C065 03279
October-
November
1977

BENJAMIN BRITTEN (1913-1976)

owen wingrave

London December 1970	Role of Kate Harper, Vyvyan, Fisher, Pears, Douglas, Shirley-Quirk Wandsworth Choir ECO Britten	LP: Decca SET 501-502 LP: London OSA 1291 CD: Decca 433 2002 Unpublished video recording also made at this time

the rape of lucretia

Snape July 1970	Role of Lucretia Harper, Pears, Luxon, Shirley-Quirk ECO Britten	LP: Decca SET 492-493 LP: London OSA 1288 CD: Decca 425 6662 Excerpts LP: Decca SET 537

spring symphony

London 28-29 June 1978	Armstrong, Tear St.Clement Danes Choir LSO Chorus LSO Previn	LP: EMI ASD 3650/1C063 03363 CD: EMI CDM 764 7362

phaedra

Petersham March 1977	ECO Bedford	LP: Decca SXL 6847 CD: Decca 425 6662

corpus christi carol/a boy was born

London 9-10 February 1967	Moore	LP: EMI HQS 1091/ESD 100 6421/SLS 5275 LP: Angel 36456 CD: EMI CDM 565 0092

ANTON BRUCKNER (1824-1896)

te deum

London 12 January 1961	Harper, Lewis, Nowakowski BBC SO and Chorus Klemperer	LP: Melodram MEL 214

WILLIAM BUSCH (1901-1945)

rest

London 9-10 February 1967	Moore	LP: EMI HQS 1091/ESD 100 6421 LP: Angel 36456 CD: EMI CDM 565 0092

GIULIO CACCINI (1545-1618)

amarilli mia bella!

London January 1978	ASMIF Marriner	LP: Philips 9500 557 CD: Philips 434 1732

ANTONIO CALDARA (1670-1736)

come raggio di sol; sebben crudele me fai languir; selve amiche

London January 1978	ASMIF Marriner	LP: Philips 9500 557 CD: Philips 434 1732

THOMAS CAMPION (1567-1620)

never love unless you can; oft have i sighed; if thou longst so much to learn; fair would i wed

London	Instrumentalists	LP: EMI HQS 1091/ESD 100 6421
9-10		LP: Angel 36456
February		Fair would I wed
1967		LP: EMI SEOM 8/SLS 5275

FRANCESCO CAVALLI (1602-1676)

la calisto, arranged by leppard

Glyndebourne	Role of Diana	LP: Decca ZNF 11-12
10-13	Cotrubas, Cahill,	CD: Decca 436 2162
August	Kubiak, Cuenod,	Excerpts
1971	Gottlieb, Trama	LP: Decca GRV 5
	Glyndebourne	CD: Decca 440 4132
	Festival Chorus	
	LPO	
	Leppard	

ANTONIO CESTI (1623-1669)

intorno all' idol mio

London	ASMIF	LP: Philips 9500 557
January	Marriner	CD: Philips 434 1732
1978		

EMMANUEL CHABRIER (1841-1894)

vilanelle

London	Moore	LP: EMI ASD 2929/ESD 102 4391/1C063 02439
13-16		
October		
1972		

ERNEST CHAUSSON (1855-1899)

poème de l'amour et de la mer

London 17 April 1975	LSO Svetlanov	CD: BBC Radio Classics 569 1742
London April 1977	LSO Previn	LP: EMI ASD 3455/1C063 02963 CD: EMI CZS 568 6672

chanson perpétuelle

London June 1966	Melos Ensemble	LP: Decca OL 298/SOL 298/GRV5 CD: Decca 440 4132

PETER CORNELIUS (1824-1874)

duets: heimatgedanken; verratene liebe; ich und du; der beste liebesbrief

London 21-23 August 1969	Fischer-Dieskau Barenboim	LP: EMI ASD 2553/1C063 02041

HENRY WALFORD DAVIES (1869-1941)

god be in my head

Cambridge 30-31 October 1980	Ledger	LP: EMI ASD 3981

CLAUDE DEBUSSY (1862-1918)

3 chansons de bilitis; le promenoir des 2 amants

London July 1969	Moore	LP: EMI ASD 2590 <u>Excerpts</u> LP: EMI SLS 5275

MAURICE DELAGE (1879-1961)

4 poèmes hindous

London June 1966	Melos Ensemble Keefe	LP: Decca OL 298/SOL 298 CD: Decca 440 4132

FREDERICK DELIUS (1862-1934)

songs of sunset

Liverpool June 1968	Shirley-Quirk Liverpool Philharmonic Orchestra & Chorus Groves	LP: EMI ASD 2437 LP: Angel 36603 CD: EMI CMS 764 2182

GAETONO DONIZETTI (1797-1848)

maria stuarda

London 1-22 April 1982	Role of Maria Plowright, Rendall, Opie, Tomlinson ENO Orchestra and Chorus Mackerras Sung in English	LP: EMI SLS 5277 LP: Angel 3927 CD: EMI CMS 769 3722
London April 1982	Plowright, Rendall, Opie, Tomlinson ENO Orchestra and Chorus Mackerras Sung in English	VHS Video: Castle CVI 2038

JOHN DOWLAND (1563-1626)

come again

| London
9-10
February
1967 | Instrumentalists | LP: EMI HQS 1091/ESD 100 6421/SLS 5275
LP: Angel 36456 |

THOMAS DUNHILL (1877-1946)

the cloths of heaven; to the queen of my heart

| London
1962 | Isepp | LP: Saga XIP 7013/XID 5213/STXID 5213
CD: Saga SCD 9012 |

HENRI DUPARC (1848-1933)

au pays ou se fait la guerre

| London July 1969 | Moore | LP: EMI ASD 2590/SLS 5275 |

| London April 1977 | LSO Previn | LP: EMI ASD 3455/1C063 02963
CD: EMI CZS 568 6672 |

l'invitation au voyage

| London April 1977 | LSO Previn | LP: EMI ASD 3455/1C063 02963
CD: EMI CZS 568 6672 |

le manoir de rosemonde

| London April 1977 | LSO Previn | LP: EMI ASD 3455/1C063 02963
CD: EMI CZS 568 6672 |

phidylé

| London July 1969 | Moore | LP: EMI ASD 2590 |

| London April 1977 | LSO Previn | LP: EMI ASD 3455/1C063 02963
CD: EMI CZS 568 6672 |

la vie antérieure

| London April 1977 | LSO Previn | LP: EMI ASD 3455/1C063 02963
CD: EMI CZS 568 6672 |

FRANCESCO DURANTE (1684-1755)

danza fanciulla gentile

London January 1978	ASMIF Marriner	LP: Philips 9500 557 CD: Philips 434 1732

MAURICE DURUFLE (1902-1986)

requiem

Cambridge 30 October 1980	Roberts Kings College Choir ECO Ledger	LP: EMI ASD 4086/1C065 43143

WERNER EGK (1901-1983)

la tentation de sainte antoine

Munich November 1965	Members of Bavarian RO and Koeckert Quartet	LP: DG SLPM 139 142 CD: DG 449 0972

EDWARD ELGAR (1857-1934)

the dream of gerontius

Manchester
27-30
December
1964
	Lewis, Borg
	Ambrosian Singers
	Sheffield and
	Hallé Choirs
	Hallé Orchestra
	Barbirolli
		LP: EMI ALP 2101-2102/ASD 648-649/RLS 770/
		   SLS 770/1C163 00272-00273
		LP: Angel 3660
		CD: EMI CMS 763 1852
		Excerpts
		LP: EMI SLS 796/SLS 5275/SEOM 7/SEOM 11/
		   YKM 5013/CFP 4548
		CD: EMI CDCFP 4548

Warwick 6-8 September 1986	Mitchinson, Shirley-Quirk CBSO Choir CBSO Rattle	LP: EMI EX 749 5491 CD: EMI CDS 749 5492

sea pictures

London 30 August 1965	LSO Barbirolli	LP: EMI ALP 2106/ASD 655/ASD 2721/ SLS 5013/1C063 02163 LP: Angel 36796 CD: EMI CDC 747 3292/CMS 763 1852 Excerpts LP: EMI SLS 5275
London 9 September 1982	BBC SO Loughran	CD: BBC Radio Classics 569 1672

the music makers

London 21-23 December 1966	LPO Choir LPO Boult	LP: EMI ALP 2311/ASD 2311/ED 29 12741 LP: Vanguard VSD 71225 LP: London Philharmonic Orchestra LPJ 50 CD: EMI CDC 749 0222/CDM 565 1072/ CDS 747 2088

160th Season   Second Concert of Series

PROGRAMME   3 NOVEMBER 1971   8 pm

PRELUDE: TRISTAN AND ISOLDE
(Concert ending)
Wagner

FIVE WESENDONK SONGS
Wagner

SYMPHONY No. 7 IN E
Bruckner

BBC SYMPHONY ORCHESTRA
(Leader: Eli Goren)

REGINALD GOODALL
JANET BAKER

Royal Philharmonic Society concert

165th Season   **Last Concert of Series**

PROGRAMME   11 MAY 1977   8 pm

MASS IN B MINOR
Bach

LONDON PHILHARMONIC ORCHESTRA
Leader: David Nolan

CARLO MARIA GIULINI

SHEILA ARMSTRONG   JANET BAKER
ROBERT TEAR   NORMAN BAILEY

LONDON PHILHARMONIC CHOIR
Chorus Master: John Alldis

Royal Philharmonic Society concert

GABRIEL FAURE (1845-1924)

la chanson d'ève, song cycle

| London 13-14 August 1988 | Parsons | CD: Hyperion CDA 66320 |

après un rêve

| London 13-14 August 1988 | Parsons | CD: Hyperion CDA 66320 |

aubade

| London 13-14 August 1988 | Parsons | CD: Hyperion CDA 66320 |

aurore

| London 13-14 August 1988 | Parsons | CD: Hyperion CDA 66320 |

automne

| London 19 July 1969 | Moore | LP: EMI ASD 2590
CD: EMI CDM 565 0092 |

barcarolle

| London 13-14 August 1988 | Parsons | CD: Hyperion CDA 66320 |

les berceaux

London 13-14 August 1988	Parsons	CD: Hyperion CDA 66320

chanson de pêcheur

London 19 July 1969	Moore	LP: EMI ASD 2590 CD: EMI CDM 565 0092
London 13-14 August 1988	Parsons	CD: Hyperion CDA 66320

clair de lune

London 19 July 1969	Moore	LP: EMI ASD 2590/SEOM 8/SLS 5275 CD: EMI CDM 565 0092

en prière

London 13-14 August 1988	Parsons	CD: Hyperion CDA 66320

en sourdine

London 19 July 1969	Moore	LP: EMI ASD 2590 CD: EMI CDM 565 0092
Snape 14 June 1971	Leppard	CD: BBC Music Magazine BBCMM 143
London 13-14 August 1988	Parsons	CD: Hyperion CDA 66320

36 Baker

fleur jetée

London 19 July 1969	Moore	LP: EMI ASD 2590/SLS 5275 CD: EMI CDM 565 0092
Snape 14 June 1971	Leppard	CD: BBC Music Magazine BBCMM 143

green

London 13-14 August 1988	Parsons	CD: Hyperion CDA 66320

hymne

London 13-14 August 1988	Parsons	CD: Hyperion CDA 66320

mai

London 19 July 1969	Moore	LP: EMI ASD 2590 CD: EMI CDM 565 0092
London 13-14 August 1988	Parsons	CD: Hyperion CDA 66320

mandoline

Snape 14 June 1971	Leppard	CD: BBC Music Magazine BBCMM 143
London 13-14 August 1988	Parsons	CD: Hyperion CDA 66320

notre amour

London   Moore   LP: EMI ASD 2590
19 July   CD: EMI CDM 565 0092
1969

les présents

London   Parsons   CD: Hyperion CDA 66320
13-14
August
1988

prison

London   Moore   LP: EMI ASD 2590
19 July   CD: EMI CDM 565 0092
1971

rêve d'amour

London   Parsons   CD: Hyperion CDA 66320
13-14
August
1988

les roses d'isphahan

London   Parsons   CD: Hyperion CDA 66320
13-14
August
1988

38 Baker

le secret

London 13-14 August 1988	Parsons	CD: Hyperion CDA 66320

soir

London 19 July 1969	Moore	LP: EMI ASD 2590 CD: EMI CDM 565 0092
Snape 14 June 1971	Leppard	CD: BBC Music Magazine BBCMM 143

spleen

London 13-14 August 1988	Parsons	CD: Hyperion CDA 66320

toujours/poèmes d'un jour

London 13-14 August 1988	Parsons	CD: Hyperion CDA 66320

GERALD FINZI (1901-1956)

come away death!

London 1962	Isepp	LP: Saga XIP 7013/XID 5213/STXID 5213 CD: Saga SCD 9012

it was a lover and his lass

London 1962	Isepp	LP: Saga XIP 7013/XID 5213/STXID 5213 CD: Saga SCD 9012
London 13-16 October 1972	Moore	LP: EMI ASD 2929/ESD 102 4391/1C063 02439

DONALD FORD (20th century)

a prayer to our lady

Cambridge 30-31 October 1980	Ledger	LP: EMI ASD 3981

CECIL ARMSTRONG GIBBS (1889-1960)

there is a sacred city; love is a sickness

London 1962	Isepp	LP: Saga XIP 7013/XID 5213/STXID 5213 CD: Saga SCD 9012

TOMMASO GIORDANI (1733-1806)

caro mio ben

London January 1978	ASMIF Marriner	LP: Philips 9500 557 CD: Philips 434 1732

CHRISTOPH WILLIBALD GLUCK (1714-1787)

orfeo ed euridice

London 11 August 1982	Role of Orfeo Gale, Speiser Glyndebourne Festival Chorus LPO Leppard	CD: Music and Arts CD 295 Excerpts CD: IMP DMCD 98
Brent 12-18 August 1982	Gale, Speiser Glyndebourne Festival Chorus LPO Leppard	LP: Erato NUM 75042 CD: Erato 2292 458642 Excerpts CD: Erato 4509 985122/0630 138059
Glyndebourne 22 August 1982	Gale, Speiser Glyndebourne Festival Chorus LPO Leppard	VHS Video: Castle CVI 2035

orfeo ed euridice, excerpts (che puro ciel!; che farò)

London April 1975	ECO Leppard	LP: Philips 9500 023/6570 829/6767 001 CD: Philips 422 9502

armide, excerpt (le perfide renaud me fuit!)

London	ECO	LP: Philips 9500 023/6767 001
April	Leppard	CD: Philips 422 9502
1975		

alceste, excerpt (divinités du styx!)

London	ECO	LP: Philips 9500 023/6570 829/6767 001
April	Leppard	CD: Philips 422 9502
1975		

iphigénie en aulide, excerpts (par la crainte; adieu, conservez dans votre âme)

London	ECO	LP: Philips 9500 023/6570 829/6767 001
April	Leppard	CD: Philips 422 9502
1975		

iphigénie en tauride, excerpt (non cet affreux devoir!)

London	ECO	LP: Philips 9500 023/6570 829/6767 001
April	Leppard	CD: Philips 422 9502
1975		

paride ed elena, excerpt (o del mio dolce ardor)

London	ECO	LP: Philips 9500 023/6767 001
April	Leppard	CD: Philips 422 9502
1975		

CHARLES GOUNOD (1818-1893)

sérénade

Snape 14 June 1971	Leppard	CD: BBC Music Magazine BBCMM 143
London 13-16 October 1972	Moore	LP: EMI ASD 2929/1C063 02439/ESD 102 4391

BONIFAZIO GRAZIANI (1604-1664)

velut palma, cantata

Snape 14 June 1971	Leppard	CD: BBC Music Magazine BBCMM 143

IVOR GURNEY (1890-1937)

sleep

London 1962	Isepp	LP: Saga XIP 7013/XID 5213/STXID 5213 CD: Saga SCD 9012

the fields are full

London 9-10 February 1967	Moore	LP: EMI HQS 1091/ESD 100 6421 LP: Angel 36456 CD: EMI CDM 565 0092

i will go with my father a-ploughing

London 1962	Isepp	LP: Saga XIP 7013/XID 5213/ STXID 5213/5349 CD: Saga SCD 9012

REYNALDO HAHN (1875-1947)

l'heure exquise

London 13-16 October 1972	Moore	LP: EMI ASD 2929/1C063 02439/ESD 102 4391

GEORGE FRIDERIC HANDEL (1685-1759)

messiah

London 29 June- 9 August 1966	Harwood, Tear, Herincx Ambrosian Singers ECO Mackerras	LP: EMI RLS 774/SLS 774/ 1C153 00635-00637 LP: Angel 3705 CD: EMI CZS 569 4492/CZS 762 7482 Excerpts LP: EMI HQS 1244/1C053 01881/SLS 5275 CD: EMI CMS 565 8512

dixit dominus

London August 1965	Zylis-Gara, Lane, Tear, Shirley-Quirk Kings College Choir ECO Willcocks	LP: EMI ALP 2262/ASD 2262/1C053 00291/ SXLP 30444 LP: Angel 36331 CD: EMI CDM 565 3362

salve regina

London October 1978	Watts, Tear, Luxon, Shirley-Quirk London Voices ECO Leppard	CD: Erato 2292 459942

judas maccabaeus

Watford 4-12 April 1976	Palmer, Esswood, Davies, Keyte, Shirley-Quirk Wandsworth Choir ECO Mackerras	LP: DG 2710 021/413 9091 CD: DG 447 6922

italian cantata no 1 "ah crudel nel pianto mio", arranged by leppard

London	ECO	LP: EMI ASD 2468
November-	Leppard	LP: Angel 36569
December		Excerpts
1967		LP: EMI SEOM 8/SLS 5275

italian cantata no 13 "armida abbandonata", arranged by leppard

London	ECO	LP: EMI ASD 2468
November-	Leppard	LP: Angel 36569
December		
1967		

duets: giù nei tarterei regni v'andrem; quando il calma ride il mare

London	Fischer-Dieskau	LP: EMI ASD 2710
February	Instrumentalists	LP: Angel 36712
1970		

lucrezia, cantata

London	ECO	LP: Philips 6500 523/6767 001
18-22	Leppard	CD: Philips 426 4502
December		
1972		

ariodante

London	Role of Ariodante	LP: Philips 6769 025
7-21	Mathis, Burrowes,	CD: Philips 442 0962
December	Rendall, Bowman	Excerpts
1978	Ramey	LP: Philips 6570 829
	London Voices	CD: Philips 426 4502
	ECO	
	Leppard	

atalanta, excerpt (cara selve)

London 18-22 December 1972	ECO Leppard	LP: Philips 6500 523/6570 829/6767 001 CD: Philips 426 4502

hercules, excerpt (where shall i fly?)

London 18-22 December 1972	ECO Leppard	LP: Philips 6500 523/6767 001 CD: Philips 426 4502

giulio cesare

London August 1981	Role of Cesare Masterson, S.Walker, D.Jones, Bowman, Tomlinson ENO Orchestra and Chorus Mackerras Sung in English	LP: EMI EX 27 02323 CD: EMI CMS 769 7602
London 1980-1981	Masterson, S.Walker, D.Jones, Bowman, Tomlinson ENO Orchestra and Chorus Mackerras Sung in English	VHS Video: Pioneer PLMCD 771 VHS Video: Polygram 079 2463 VHS Video: MCEG VVD 383

joshua, excerpt (o had i jubal's lyre!)

Snape 14 June 1971	Leppard	CD: BBC Music Magazine BBCMM 143
London 18-22 December 1972	ECO Leppard	LP: Philips 6500 523/6570 829/6767 001 CD: Philips 426 4502

rodelinda

London 1959	Role of Eduige Sutherland, Herincx Philomusica and Chorus Farncombe	CD: Memories HR 4577

rodelinda, excerpt (dove sei?)

London 18-22 December 1972	ECO Leppard	LP: Philips 6500 523/6767 001 CD: Philips 426 4502

samson

London October 1978	Burrowes, Lott, Watts, Tear, Langridge, Oliver, Shirley-Quirk London Voices ECO Leppard	LP: Erato STU 71240

serse, excerpt (ombra mai fu)

London 18-22 December 1972	ECO Leppard	LP: Philips 6500 523/6570 829/6767 001 CD: Philips 426 4502

48 Baker

FRANZ JOSEF HAYDN (1732-1809)

scena di berenice

London 1973	ECO Leppard	LP: Philips 6500 660/6767 001

arianna a naxos

London 1973	ECO Leppard	LP: Philips 6500 660/6767 001

scottish folksong settings: the brisk young lad; o bonny lass; the white cockade; john anderson; the ploughman; duncan gray; my boy tammy; shepherds; up in the morning early; green grow the rashes; love will find out the way; sleepy bodie; o can you sew cushions; the birks of abergeldie; my ain kind dearie; i'm o'er young to marry yet; cumbernauld house

London 1975	G.Malcolm, Menuhin, Pople	LP: EMI ASD 3167/1C063 02709 O can you sew cushions LP: EMI SLS 5275

MICHAEL HEAD (1900-1976)

a piper

London 1962	Isepp	LP: Saga XIP 7013/XID 5213/STXID 5213 CD: Saga SCD 9012

GUSTAV HOLST (1874-1934)

choral fantasia

London 1963	Purcell Singers ECO I.Holst	LP: EMI HQS 1260/1C053 01146 LP: World Records CM 50/SCM 50 LP: Everest SDBR 3136 CD: EMI CDM 565 5852

savitri, chamber opera

London October 1965	Tear, Hemsley Purcell Singers ECO I.Holst	LP: Decca NF 6/ZNF 6
London October 1965	Tear, Hemsley Purcell Singers ECO I.Holst	CD: Intaglio INCD 7451

HERBERT HOWELLS (1892-1983)

king david; come sing and dance

London 1962	Isepp	LP: Saga XIP 7013/XID 5213/STXID 5213 CD: Saga SCD 9012

PELHAM HUMFREY (1647-1674)

wilt thou forgive that sin?

Snape 14 June 1971	Leppard, Hall	CD: BBC Music Magazine BBCMM 143

JOHN IRELAND (1879-1962)

a thanksgiving; her song

London 1962	Isepp	LP: Saga XIP 7013/XID 5213/STXID 5213 CD: Saga SCD 9012

down by the salley gardens

London 9-10 February 1967	Moore	LP: EMI HQS 1091/ESD 100 6421 LP: Angel 36456 CD: EMI CDM 565 0092/CDM 764 7162
London 13-16 October 1972	Moore	LP: EMI ASD 2929/ESD 102 4391/1C063 02439

HENRY LAWES (1596-1662)

a dialogue on a kiss

London February 1970	Fischer-Dieskau Instrumentalists	LP: EMI ASD 2710 LP: Angel 36712

WILLIAM LAWES (1602-1645)

a dialogue between daphne and strephon; a dialogue between charon and philomel

London February 1970	Fischer-Dieskau Instrumentalists	LP: EMI ASD 2710 LP: Angel 36712 <u>Daphne and Strephon</u> LP: EMI SLS 5275

SAMUEL LIDDLE (1867-1951)

how lovely are thy dwellings; the lord is my shepherd; abide with me

Cambridge 30-31 October 1980	Ledger	LP: EMI ASD 3981

FRANCISZEK LILIUS (1600-1657)

tua jesu dilecto

London February 1970	Fischer-Dieskau Instrumentalists	LP: EMI ASD 2710 LP: Angel 36712

FRANZ LISZT (1811-1886)

lieder: die lorelei; s'il est un charmant gazon; du bist wie eine blume; im rhein im schönen strome; über allen gipfeln; der du von dem himmel bist; es war ein könig in thule; freudvoll und leidvoll; die 3 zigeuner; das veilchen; die vätergruft; die fischertöchter

London 7 June 1979- 3 April 1980	Parsons	LP: EMI ASD 3906/1C063 03825 <u>Es war ein König in Thule</u> LP: EMI SLS 5275

ANTONIO LOTTI (1667-1740)

pur dicesti o bocca bella

London January 1978	ASMIF Marriner	LP: Philips 9500 557 CD: Philips 434 1732

GUSTAV MAHLER (1860-1911)

das lied von der erde

Cleveland February 1970	Lewis Cleveland Orchestra Szell	CD: Cleveland Orchestra TC 093-75
Amsterdam 1-3 September 1975	King Concertgebouw Orchestra Haitink	LP: Philips 6500 831/412 9271 CD: Philips 439 2792/454 0142
Manchester 22 February 1977	Mitchinson BBC Philharmonic Leppard	CD: BBC Radio Classics BBCRD 9120
Munich 1975	Kmennt Bavarian RO Kubelik	CD: Originals SH 806-807

symphony no 2 "resurrection"

London 30 July 1963	Woodland Goldsmiths, BBC & LSO Choirs LSO Stokowski	LP: Penzance PR 19 CD: Intaglio INCD 7491 CD: Music and Arts CD 885
Munich 29 January 1965	Harper Bavarian Radio Orchestra & Chorus Klemperer	CD: Nuova era NE 6714 CD: Arkadia CD 703/CDGI 703 CD: Documents LV 937 CD: EMI CDM 566 8672
St Albans 31 August- 2 September 1973	Armstrong LSO Chorus LSO Bernstein	LP: CBS 32681/78249 CD: Sony SM2K 47573
Watford 27 April- 1 June 1986	Auger CBSO Chorus CBSO Rattle	LP: EMI EL 27 05983 CD: EMI CDS 747 9268

symphony no 3

London 22 November 1987	LSO Chorus LSO Tilson Thomas	CD: Sony M2K 44553

das klagende lied

London 20 July 1981	Cahill, Tear, Howell BBC Chorus BBCSO Rozhdestvensky	CD: BBC Radio Classics 569 1412

kindertotenlieder

Manchester May-July 1967	Hallé Barbirolli	LP: EMI ASD 2338/SLS 5013/SLS 5275/ 1C063 00347/SHZE 338 LP: Angel 36465 CD: EMI CDC 747 7932/CZS 762 7072
Tel Aviv October 1974	Israel PO Bernstein	LP: CBS 33532/79355

lieder eines fahrenden gesellen

Manchester May-July 1967	Hallé Barbirolli	LP: EMI ASD 2338/SLS 5013/SLS 5275/ 1C063 00347 LP: Angel 36465 CD: EMI CDC 747 7932/CZS 762 7072
London 24-25 February 1983	Parsons	CD: Hyperion CDA 66100

ADMINISTRATEUR GÉNÉRAL BERNARD LEFORT

mardi 18 et mercredi 19 novembre 1980

Concert Symphonique
Direction : **Raymond Leppard**
Soliste : **Dame Janet Baker**
Orchestre National de l'Opéra

Félix Mendelssohn-Bartholdy Troisième Symphonie en la mineur
(1809-1847) opus 56. « Écossaise. » (1842)
*Andante con moto - Allegro un poco agitato -
Vivace non troppo - Adagio -
Allegro vivacissimo - Allegro maestoso assai -*

Infelice. Opus 94, air de concert. (1843)
soliste : Dame Janet Baker

Entracte

Georg Friedrich Hændel *Fireworks* - **Feux d'Artifice.** (1749)
(1685-1759) *Ouverture - Bourée - La Paix -
La Réjouissance - Menuet I et II -*

Lucrezia, « O Numi eterni », cantate
Éditée et réalisée par Raymond Leppard
Soliste : Dame Janet Baker

ROYAL FESTIVAL HALL

General Manager: T. E. Bean, C.B.E.

PHILHARMONIA CONCERT SOCIETY LTD

ARTISTIC DIRECTOR:
WALTER LEGGE

PHILHARMONIA ORCHESTRA

PRINCIPAL CONDUCTOR:
OTTO KLEMPERER

LEADER: HUGH BEAN

MOZART: Symphony No. 29 in A, K.201

MAHLER: Symphony No. 2 in C minor

HEATHER HARPER   JANET BAKER

PHILHARMONIA CHORUS

CHORUS MASTER: WILHELM PITZ
CONDUCTOR OF OFFSTAGE BAND: OTTO FREUDENTHAL

OTTO KLEMPERER

Thursday, December 19, 1963, at 8 p.m.

Programme One Shilling and Sixpence

This concert is given in association with the Arts Council of Great Britain and the London County Council

ablösung im sommer/lieder und gesänge aus der jugendzeit

London 24-25 February 1983	Parsons	CD: Hyperion CDA 66100

aus! aus!/lieder und gesänge aus der jugendzeit

London 24-25 February 1983	Parsons	CD: Hyperion CDA 66100

des antonius zu padua fischpredigt/des knaben wunderhorn

Watford 28-29 March 1966	LPO Morris	LP: Delysé ECB 3177/DS 3177 LP: Angel 36380 LP: Everest SDBR 3488 LP: Decca SDD 326 CD: Nimbus NI 5084 CD: Pickwick PCD 1035/PCD 2020 CD: Carlton 30367 01542

blicke mir nicht in die lieder/rückert-lieder

Watford 16-19 July 1969	New Philharmonia Barbirolli	LP: EMI ASD 2519/ASD 2721/ASD 4409/ SLS 785/SLS 5013/1C063 01998/ 1C063 02163/1C065 02122/SLS 5275 LP: Angel 3760/36796 CD: EMI CDC 747 7932/CZS 762 7072
London 22 November 1987	LSO Tilson Thomas	CD: Sony M2K 44553

erinnerung/lieder und gesänge aus der jugendzeit

London 24-25 February 1983	Parsons	CD: Hyperion CDA 66100

frühlingsmorgen/lieder und gesänge aus der jugendzeit

London December 1968	Moore	LP: EMI SAN 255/1C065 01961 LP: Angel 36640
London 24-25 February 1983	Parsons	CD: Hyperion CDA 66100

hans und grete/lieder und gesänge aus der jugendzeit

London 24-25 February 1983	Parsons	CD: Hyperion CDA 66100

ich atmet' einen linden duft/rückert-lieder

Watford 16-19 July 1969	New Philharmonia Barbirolli	LP: EMI ASD 2519/ASD 2721/ASD 4409/ SLS 785/SLS 5013/1C063 01998/ 1C063 02163/1C065 02122 LP: Angel 3760/36796 CD: EMI CDC 747 7932/CZS 762 7072
London 22 November 1987	LSO Tilson Thomas	CD: Sony M2K 44553

ich bin der welt abhanden gekommen/rückert-lieder

Manchester May-July 1967	Hallé Barbirolli	LP: EMI ASD 2338/SEOM 8/1C063 01988/ 1C063 00347/1C065 02122 LP: Angel 36465
Watford 16-19 July 1969	New Philharmonia Barbirolli	LP: EMI ASD 2519/ASD 2721/ASD 4409/ 1C063 02163/SLS 785/SLS 5013/SLS 5275 LP: Angel 3760/36796 CD: EMI CDC 747 7932/CZS 762 7072
London 22 November 1987	LSO Tilson Thomas	CD: Sony M2K 44553

ich ging mit lust/lieder und gesänge aus der jugendzeit

London   Parsons   CD: Hyperion CDA 66100
24-25
February
1983

im lenz

London   Parsons   CD: Hyperion CDA 66100
24-25
February
1983

das irdische leben/des knaben wunderhorn

Watford   LPO   LP: Delysé ECB 3177/DS 3177
28-29   Morris   LP: Angel 36380
March   LP: Everest SDBR 3488
1966   LP: Decca SDD 326
                                     CD: Nimbus NI 5084
                                     CD: Pickwick PCD 1035/PCD 2020
                                     CD: Carlton 30367 01542

liebst du um schönheit/rückert-lieder

Watford
16-19
July
1969
	New Philharmonia
	Barbirolli
		LP: EMI ASD 2519/ASD 2721/ASD 4409/
		      SLS 785/SLS 5013/1C063 01998/
		      1C063 02163/1C065 02122
		LP: Angel 3760/36796
		CD: EMI CDC 747 7932/CZS 762 7072

London 22 November 1987	LSO Tilson Thomas	CD: Sony M2K 44553

nicht wiedersehen!/lieder und gesänge aus der jugendzeit

London 24-25 February 1983	Parsons	CD: Hyperion CDA 66100

phantasie aus don juan/lieder und gesänge aus der jugendzeit

London 24-25 February 1983	Parsons	CD: Hyperion CDA 66100

rheinlegendchen/des knaben wunderhorn

Watford 28-29 March 1966	LPO Morris	LP: Delysé ECB 3177/DS 3177 LP: Angel 36380 LP: Everest SDBR 3488 LP: Decca SDD 326/SDD 368 CD: Nimbus NI 5084 CD: Pickwick PCD 1035/PCD 2020 CD: Carlton 30367 01542

60 Baker

scheiden und meiden/lieder und gesänge aus der jugendzeit

London December 1968	Moore	LP: EMI SAN 255/1C065 01961 LP: Angel 36640
London 24-25 February 1983	Parsons	CD: Hyperion CDA 66100

selbstgefühl/lieder und gesänge aus der jugendzeit

London 24-25 Febuary 1983	Parsons	CD: Hyperion CDA 66100

serenade aus don juan/lieder und gesänge aus der jugendzeit

London 24-25 February 1983	Parsons	CD: Hyperion CDA 66100

starke einbildungskraft/lieder und gesänge aus der jugendzeit

London 24-25 February 1983	Parsons	CD: Hyperion CDA 66100

trost im unglück/des knaben wunderhorn

Watford	LPO	LP: Delysé ECB 3177/DS 3177
28-29	Morris	LP: Angel 36380
March		LP: Everest SDBR 3488
1966		LP: Decca SDD 326
		CD: Nimbus NI 5084
		CD: Pickwick PCD 1035/PCD 2020
		CD: Carlton 30367 01542

um mitternacht/rückert-lieder

Watford	New Philharmonia	LP: EMI ASD 2519/ASD 2721/ASD 4409/
16-19	Barbirolli	SLS 785/SLS 5013/1C063 01998/
July		1C063 02163/1C065 02122
1969		LP: Angel 3760/36796
		CD: EMI CDC 747 7932/CZS 762 7072

London	LSO	CD: Sony M2K 44553
22 November	Tilson Thomas	
1987		

um schlimme kinder artig zu machen/lieder und gesänge aus der jugendzeit

London	Parsons	CD: Hyperion CDA 66100
24-25		
February		
1983		

verlor'ne müh/des knaben wunderhorn

Watford	LPO	LP: Delysé ECB 3177/DS 3177
28-29	Morris	LP: Angel 36380
March		LP: Everest SDBR 3488
1966		LP: Decca SDD 326
		CD: Nimbus NI 5084
		CD: Pickwick PCD 1035/PCD 2020
		CD: Carlton 30367 01542

62 Baker

winterlied

London 24-25 February 1983	Parsons	CD: Hyperion CDA 66100

wo die schönen trompeten blasen/des knaben wunderhorn

Watford   LPO   LP: Delysé ECB 3177/DS 3177
28-29   Morris   LP: Angel 36380
March   LP: Everest SDBR 3488
1966   LP: Decca SDD 326/SDD 368
                              CD: Nimbus NI 5084
                              CD: Pickwick PCD 1035/PCD 2020
                              CD: Carlton 30367 01542

zu strassburg auf der schanz/lieder und gesänge aus der jugendzeit

London   Parsons   CD: Hyperion CDA 66100
24-25
February
1983

EASTHOPE MARTIN (1882-1925)

the holy child

Cambridge 30-31 October 1980	Ledger	LP: EMI ASD 3981

JOHANN PAUL MARTINI (1741-1816)

plaisir d'amour

London January 1978	ASMIF Marriner	LP: Philips 9500 557 CD: Philips 434 1732

JULES MASSENET (1842-1912)

crépuscule

London 13-16 December 1972	Moore	LP: EMI ASD 2929/1C063 02439

FELIX MENDELSSOHN-BARTHOLDY (1809-1847)

elijah

London
1-9
July
1968
	Jones, Gedda,
	Fischer-Dieskau
	Wandsworth Choir
	New Philharmonia
	Orchestra & Chorus
	Frühbeck de Burgos
		LP: EMI SLS 935/1C165 00107-00109/
		     1C149 00107-00109
		LP: Angel 3738
		CD: EMI CZS 568 6012
		Excerpts
		LP: EMI ASD 2609/SEOM 8/1 C063 00908/
		     1C063 01970

psalm 42

London September 1989	LSO Chorus City of London Sinfonia Hickox	CD: Virgin CDC 59589/VBD 561 4692

infelice, concert aria

London September 1989	City of London Sinfonia Hickox	CD: Virgin CDC 59589/VBD 561 4692

ye spotted snakes/a midsummer night's dream

London	Harper	LP: Columbia 33CX 1746/SAX 2393
28 January-	Philharmonia	LP: Columbia (Germany) C 91131/STC 91131/
16 February	Orchestra & Chorus	33WCX 524/SAXW 9541
1960	Klemperer	LP: Columbia (France) 33FCX 838/SAXF 190
		LP: Columbia (Italy) 33QCX 10427/SAXQ 7327
		LP: Angel 35881
		LP: EMI SXLP 30196/1C053 00521
		CD: EMI CDC 747 2302/CDM 764 1442

duets: abschiedslied der zugvögel; wie kann ich froh und lustig sein?; herbstlied; suleika und hatem

London	Fischer-Dieskau	LP: EMI ASD 2553/1C063 02041
21-23	Barenboim	
August		
1969		

auf flügeln des gesanges

London	Moore	LP: EMI ASD 2929/1C063 02439/ESD 100 4391
13-16		
October		
1972		

London	Parsons	LP: EMI ASD 4070
29-30		
December		
1980		

lieder: morgengruss; der blumenstrauss; neue liebe; die sterne schau'n; es weiss und rät es doch keiner; ich hör' ein vöglein singen; frage; scheidend; frühlingsglaube; herbstlied; andres maienlied; der blumenkranz; nachtlied; im grünen; reiselied

London	Parsons	LP: EMI ASD 4070
29-30		
December		
1980		

GEORGE MONRO (18th century)

my lovely celia

London 9-10 February 1967	Instrumentalists	LP: EMI HQS 1091/ESD 100 6421/SLS 5275 LP: Angel 36456

CLAUDIO MONTEVERDI (1567-1643)

il ritorno d'ulisse, arranged by leppard

London 3 August 1972	<u>Role of Penelope</u> Woodland, Howells, Lewis, Wakefield, Luxon, Lloyd Glyndebourne Festival Chorus LPO Leppard	Unpublished radio broadcast
Glyndebourne 24 August 1973	Woodland, Howells, Lewis, Wakefield, Luxon, Lloyd Glyndebourne Festival Chorus LPO Leppard	VHS Video: Pickwick SL 2005

l'incoronazione di poppea, excerpt (disprezzata regina, arranged by leppard)

London June-July 1969	ECO Leppard	LP: EMI ASD 2615/1C063 02058 SXLP 30280

l'arianna, excerpt (lasciatemi morir, arranged by leppard)

London June-July 1969	ECO Leppard	LP: EMI ASD 2615/1C063 02058 SXLP 30280/SLS 5275

quel sguardo sdegnosetto; si dolce è'l tormento; maledetto sia l'aspetto!

Snape 14 June 1971	Leppard, Hall	CD: BBC Music Magazine BBCMM 143

WOLFGANG AMADEUS MOZART (1756-1791)

requiem

London July 1971	Armstrong, Gedda, Fischer-Dieskau Alldis Choir ECO Barenboim	LP: EMI ASD 2788/1C063 02246 CD: EMI CZS 762 8922

exsultate jubilate

Edinburgh July 1984	Scottish CO Leppard	LP: Erato NUM 75176 CD: Erato ECD 88090

così fan tutte

Watford 19 May- 2 June 1974	Role of Dorabella Caballé, Cotrubas, Gedda, Van Allan, Ganzarolli Covent Garden Orchestra & Chorus Davis	LP: Philips 6707 025/6747 385/6747 280 CD: Philips 416 6332/422 5422/456 3752 Excerpts CD: Philips 446 2462/462 4622

la clemenza di tito

Watford 14-22 July 1976	Role of Vitellia Popp, Stade, Minton, Burrows, Lloyd Covent Garden Orchestra & Chorus Davis	LP: Philips 6703 079/6747 386 CD: Philips 420 0972/422 5442

la clemenza di tito, excerpt (deh per questo istante solo)

London	ECO	LP: Philips 6500 660/6570 829/6767 001
1973	Leppard	

la clemenza di tito, excerpt (parto, parto!)

Edinburgh	Scottish CO	LP: Erato NUM 75156
July	Leppard	CD: Erato ECD 88090
1984		

idomeneo, excerpt (ch'io mi scordi di te?)

Edinburgh	Scottish CO	LP: Erato NUM 75156
July	Leppard	CD: Erato ECD 88090
1984		

le nozze di figaro, excerpts (alternative arias: al desio di chi t'adora; un moto di gioia)

Edinburgh	Scottish CO	LP: Erato NUM 75156
July	Leppard	CD: Erato ECD 88090
1984		

concert arias: vado ma dove?; chi sà, chi sà, qual sia

Edinburgh	Scottish CO	LP: Erato NUM 75156
July	Leppard	CD: Erato ECD 88090
1984		

lieder: abendempfindung; das veilchen

London	Leppard	LP: Philips 6500 660/6767 001
1973		

GIOVANNI PAISIELLO (1740-1816)

ne cor più non mi sento

London	ASMIF	LP: Philips 9500 557
January	Marriner	CD: Philips 434 1732
1978		

HUBERT PARRY (1848-1918)

proud maisie; o mistress mine

London	Moore	LP: EMI HQS 1091/ESD 100 6421
9-10		LP: Angel 36456
February		CD: EMI CDM 565 0092
1967		

jerusalem

Cambridge	Ledger	LP: EMI ASD 3981
30-31		
October		
1980		

GIOVANNI PERGOLESI (1710-1736)

magnificat

Cambridge	Vaughan, Partridge,	LP: Decca RG 505/ZRG 505
July	Keyte	CD: Decca 425 7242/455 0172
1966	Kings College	
	Choir	
	ASMIF	
	Willcocks	

ogni pena più spietata

London	ASMIF	LP: Philips 9500 557
January	Marriner	CD: Philips 434 1732
1978		

NICCOLO PICCINI (1728-1800)

o notte o dea del mistero

London	ASMIF	LP: Philips 9500 557
January	Marriner	CD: Philips 434 1732
1978		

MARY PLUMSTEAD (1905-1980)

a grateful heart; close thine eyes

Cambridge	Ledger	LP: EMI ASD 3981
30-31		
October		
1980		

HENRY PURCELL (1659-1695)

dido and aeneas

London October 1961	Role of Dido Clark, Sinclair, Herincx St Anthony Singers ECO Lewis	LP: Decca OL 50216/SOL 60047 CD: Decca 425 7202 Excerpts LP: Decca GRV 5 CD: Decca 436 4622/440 4132
Snape 1978	Burrowes, Pears London Opera Chorus Aldeburgh Orchestra Bedford	LP: Decca SET 615

duets: sound the trumpet!; my dearest my fairest; no, resistance is but vain; shepherd, leave decoying!

London 12-14 August 1969	Fischer-Dieskau Barenboim	LP: EMI ASD 2553/1C063 02041

lament from bonduca; pursuing beauty; ah cruel bloody fate!

Snape 14 June 1971	Leppard, Hall	CD: BBC Music Magazine BBCMM 143

lord, what is man?

London 9-10 February 1967	Instrumentalists	LP: EMI HQS 1091/SEOM 8/ESD 100 6421 LP: Angel 36456

ROGER QUILTER (1877-1953)

love's philosophy

London 9-10 February 1967	Moore	LP: EMI HQS 1091/ESD 100 6421/ 　　　1C053 00642/SLS 5275 LP: Angel 36456 CD: EMI CDM 565 0092

it was a lover and his lass

London 13-16 October 1972	Moore	LP: EMI ASD 2929/1C063 02439/ESD 102 4391

JEAN-PHILIPPE RAMEAU (1683-1764)

hippolyte et aricie

London July 1965	Role of Phèdre Woodland, Gomez, Tear, English, Shirley-Quirk, Stalman St Anthony Singers ECO Lewis	LP: Decca OL 286-288/SOL 286-288 CD: Decca 444 5262 Excerpts LP: Decca GRV 5 CD: Decca 440 4132

MAURICE RAVEL (1875-1937)

shéhérazade

London 27-28 December 1967	New Philharmonia Barbirolli	LP: EMI ASD 2444/SLS 5013/1C063 01867 LP: Angel 36505 CD: EMI CZS 568 6672 Excerpts LP: EMI SLS 5275

3 poèmes de stéphane mallarmé

London June 1966	Melos Ensemble Keefe	LP: Decca OL 298/SOL 298/GRV 5 CD: Decca 440 4132

chansons madécasses

London June 1966	Melos Ensemble	LP: Decca OL 298/SOL 298 CD: Decca 440 4132

OTTORINO RESPIGHI (1879-1936)

la sensitiva, cantata for voice and orchestra

London 22-24 February 1990	City of London Sinfonia Hickox	CD: Virgin CUV 61118/VBD 561 4692

aretusa for mezzo and orchestra

London November 1991	City of London Sinfonia Hickox	CD: Collins 13492

il tramonto for voice and strings

London November 1991	City of London Sinfonia Hickox	CD: Collins 13492

WILFRED SANDERSON (1878-1935)

beyond the dawn

Cambridge   Ledger   LP: EMI ASD 3981
30-31
October
1980

DOMENICO SARRI (1679-1744)

sen corre l'agnelletta

London   ASMIF   LP: Philips 9500 557
January   Marriner   CD: Philips 434 1732
1978

ALESSANDRO SCARLATTI (1660-1725)

cantata pastorale

London   ECO   LP: EMI ASD 2615/1C063 02058/SXLP 30280
June-July   Leppard   CD: EMI CDM 565 7352
1969

spesso vibra per suo gioco; già il sole dal gange; sento nel core

London   ASMIF   LP: Philips 9500 557
January   Marriner   CD: Philips 434 1732
1978

DOMENICO SCARLATTI (1685-1757)

salve regina

London June-July 1969	ECO Leppard	LP: EMI ASD 2615/1C063 02058/SXLP 30280

JOHANN SCHEIN (1586-1630)

duets: christe, der du bist tag und licht; gott der vater wohn' uns bei

London February 1970	Fischer-Dieskau Instrumentalists	LP: EMI ASD 2710 LP: Angel 36712

ARNOLD SCHOENBERG (1874-1951)

gurrelieder

Copenhagen 18 March 1968	Arroyo, Young, Patzak, Wolstad Danish Radio Orchestra & Chorus Ferencsik	LP: EMI SLS 884/1C193 02504-02505

FRANZ SCHUBERT (1797-1828)

duets: antigone und oedip; cronnan; hektors abschied; hermann und thusnelda; mignon und der harfner; selma und selmar; singübungen; szene aus faust

| Berlin
March-
April
1972 | Fischer-Dieskau
Moore | LP: DG 2530 328/2726 083
CD: DG 435 5962 |

trios: an die sonne; begräbnislied; gebet; geburtstagshymne; gott der weltschöpfer; gott im ungewitter; lebenslust; hymne an den unendlichen; der tanz

| Berlin
March-
April
1972 | Ameling, Schreier,
Fischer-Dieskau | LP: DG 2530 409/2726 083
CD: DG 435 5962 |

abendstern (was weilst du einsam an dem himmel?)

| London
6-8
November
1967 | Moore | LP: EMI ASD 2431/1C063 00391
CD: EMI CDM 565 0092/CZS 569 3892 |

die abgeblühte linde (wirst du halten, was du schwurst?)

| London
1965 | Isepp | LP: Saga XID 5277/STXID 5277
CD: Saga SCD 9001 |

der alpenjäger (willst du nicht das lämmlein hüten?)

| London
18-19
February
1987 | Johnson | CD: Hyperion CDJ 33001 |

amalia (schön wie engel voll walhallas wonne)

| London
18-19
February
1987 | Johnson | CD: Hyperion CDJ 33001 |

78 Baker

am grabe anselmos (dass ich dich verloren habe)

London	Moore	LP: EMI ASD 2431/1C063 00391
6-8		CD: EMI CDM 565 0092/CZS 569 3892
November		
1967		

an die musik (du holde kunst, in wieviel grauen stunden)

London Parsons LP: EMI ASD 4054/1C063 43033
April- CD: EMI CZS 569 3892
December
1980

an den frühling (willkommen, schöner jüngling!)

London Johnson CD: Hyperion CDJ 33001
18-19
February
1987

an den mond (füllest wieder busch und tal)

London Johnson CD: Hyperion CDJ 33001
18-19
February
1987

an die nachtigall (geuss' nicht so laut der liebentflammten lieder!)

London Moore LP: EMI SLS 812/1C187 02172-02173
August- CD: EMI CZS 569 3892
December
1970

an sylvia (was ist sylvia, saget an!)

London Parsons LP: EMI ASD 4054/1C063 43033
April- CD: EMI CZS 569 3892
December
1980

an die untergehende sonne (sonne, du sinkst, sink' in frieden!)

London August- December 1970	Moore	LP: EMI SLS 812/1C187 02172-02173 CD: EMI CZS 569 3892
Snape 14 June 1971	Leppard	CD: BBC Music Magazine BBCMM 143

auf dem wasser zu singen (mitten im schimmer der spiegelnden wellen)

London April- December 1980	Parsons	LP: EMI ASD 4054/1C063 43033 CD: EMI CZS 569 3892

auflösung (verbirg' dich, sonne!)

London 6-8 November 1967	Moore	LP: EMI ASD 2431/1C063 00391/SLS 5275 CD: EMI CDM 565 0092/CZS 569 3892

bertas lied in der nacht (nacht umhüllt mit wehendem flügel)

London August- December 1970	Moore	LP: EMI SLS 812/1C187 01272-01273 CD: EMI CZS 569 3892

delphine (ach was soll ich begehen?)

London August- December 1970	Moore	LP: EMI SLS 812/1C187 01272-01273 CD: EMI CZS 569 3892

80 Baker

du bist die ruh'

London April- December 1980	Parsons	LP: EMI ASD 4054/1C063 43033 CD: EMI CZS 569 3892

ellens gesänge (raste, krieger, krieg ist aus!; jäger, ruhe von der jagd!; ave maria)

London August- December 1970	Moore	LP: EMI SLS 812/1C187 01272-01273 CD: EMI CZS 569 3892

epistel an herrn josef von spaun (und nimmer schreibst du!)

London August- December 1970	Moore	LP: EMI SLS 8812/1C187 01272-01273 CD: EMI CZS 569 3892
Snape 14 June 1971	Leppard	CD: BBC Music Magazine BBCMM 143

erster verlust (ach wer bringt die schönen tage?)

London 18-19 February 1987	Johnson	CD: Hyperion CDJ 33001

die erwartung (hör' ich das pförtchen nicht gehen?)

London 18-19 February 1987	Johnson	CD: Hyperion CDJ 33001

der fischer (das wasser rauscht', das wasser schwoll)

London   Johnson   CD: Hyperion CDJ 33001
18-19
February
1987

der flüchtling (frisch atmet des morgens lebendiger hauch)

London   Johnson   CD: Hyperion CDJ 33001
18-19
February
1987

die forelle (in einem bächlein helle)

London   Parsons   LP: EMI ASD 4054/1C063 43033
April-   CD: EMI CZS 569 3892
December
1980

frühlingsglaube (die linden düfte sind erwacht)

London   Parsons   LP: EMI ASD 4054/1C063 43033
April-   CD: EMI CZS 569 3892
December
1980

das geheimnis (sie konnte mir kein wörtchen sagen)

London   Johnson   CD: Hyperion CDJ 33001
18-19
February
1987

der gondelfahrer (es tanzen mond und sterne)

London   Moore   LP: EMI ASD 2431/1C063 00391
6-8   CD: EMI CDM 565 0092/CZS 569 3892
November
1967

die götter griechenlands (schöne welt, wo bist du?)

| London
6-8
November
1967 | Moore | LP: EMI ASD 2431/1C063 00391/SLS 5275
CD: EMI CDM 565 0092/CZS 569 3892 |

gretchen am spinnrade (meine ruh' ist hin, mein herz ist schwer!)

| London
August-
December
1970 | Moore | LP: EMI SLS 812/1C187 02172-02173
CD: EMI CZS 569 3892 |

heidenröslein (sah ein knab' ein röslein steh'n)

| London
13 October
1972 | Moore | LP: EMI ASD 2929/ESD 102 4391/1C063 02349 |
| London
April-
December
1980 | Parsons | LP: EMI ASD 4054/1C063 43033
CD: EMI CZS 569 3892 |

heimliches lieben (o du, wenn deine lippen mich berühren)

| London
1965 | Isepp | LP: Saga XID 5277/STXID 5277
CD: Saga SCD 9001 |

hin und wieder fliegen pfeile/claudine von villa bella

| London
August-
December
1970 | Moore | LP: EMI SLS 812/1C187 02172-02173
CD: EMI CZS 569 3892 |
| Snape
14 June
1971 | Leppard | CD: BBC Music Magazine BBCMM 143 |

iphigenie (blüht denn hier an tauris strande)

London August- December 1970	Moore	LP: EMI SLS 812/1C187 02172-02173 CD: EMI CZS 569 3892

der jüngling am bache (an der quelle sass der knabe)

London 18-19 February 1987	Johnson	CD: Hyperion CDJ 33001

die junge nonne (wie braust durch die wipfel der heulende sturm)

London August- December 1970	Moore	LP: EMI SLS 812/1C187 02172-02173 CD: EMI CZS 569 3892

liebe schwärmt auf allen wegen/claudine von villa bella

London August- December 1970	Moore	LP: EMI SLS 812/1C187 02172-02173 CD: EMI CZS 569 3892
Snape 14 June 1971	Leppard	CD: BBC Music Magazine BBCMM 143

lied (es ist so angenehm, so süss)

London 18-19 February 1987	Johnson	CD: Hyperion CDJ 33001

| **163rd Season** | **Last Concert of Series** |

| PROGRAMME | 14 MAY 1975 | 8 pm |

OVERTURE: EGMONT OP. 84
Beethoven

LES NUITS D'ÉTÉ
Berlioz

SYMPHONY No. 9 IN C
Schubert

LONDON PHILHARMONIC ORCHESTRA

Leader: Rodney Friend

CARLO MARIA GIULINI

JANET BAKER

Royal Philharmonic Society concert

litanei (ruh'n in frieden alle seelen)

London April- December 1980	Parsons	LP: EMI ASD 4054/1C063 43033 CD: EMI CZS 569 3892

das mädchen (wie so innig, möcht' ich sagen)

London August- December 1970	Moore	LP: EMI SLS 812/1C187 02172-02173 CD: EMI CZS 569 3892

des mädchens klage (der eichwald brauset, die wolken zieh'n)

London August- December 1970	Moore	LP: EMI SLS 812/1C187 02172-02173 CD: EMI CZS 569 3892

die männer sind méchant (du sagtest mir es, mutter!)

London August- December 1970	Moore	LP: EMI SLS 812/1C187 02172-02173 CD: EMI CZS 569 3892

meeresstille (tiefe stille herrscht im wasser)

London 18-19 February 1987	Johnson	CD: Hyperion CDJ 33001

mignon-lieder: heiss micht nicht reden; so lasst mich scheinen; nur wer die sehnsucht kennt; kennst du das land?

London August- December 1970	Moore	LP: EMI SLS 812/1C187 02172-02173 CD: EMI CZS 569 3892

minnelied (holder klingt der vogelsang)

| London
1965 | Isepp | LP: Saga XID 5277/STXID 5277
CD: Saga SCD 9001 |

der musensohn (durch feld und wald zu schweifen)

| London
1965 | Isepp | LP: Saga XID 5277/STXID 5277
CD: Saga SCD 9001 |
| London
April-
December
1980 | Parsons | LP: EMI ASD 4054/1C063 43033
CD: EMI CZS 569 3892 |

nacht und träume (heil'ge nacht, du sinkest nieder!)

| London
April-
December
1980 | Parsons | LP: EMI ASD 4054/1C063 43033
CD: EMI CZS 569 3892 |

nähe des geliebten (ich denke dein, wenn mir der sonne schimmer)

| London
18-19
February
1987 | Johnson | CD: Hyperion CDJ 33001 |

der pilgrim (noch in meines lebens lenze)

| London
18-19
February
1987 | Johnson | CD: Hyperion CDJ 33001 |

rastlose liebe (dem schnee, dem regen, dem wind entgegen)

| London
April-
December
1980 | Parsons | LP: EMI ASD 4054/1C063 43033
CD: EMI CZS 569 3892 |

schäfers klagelied (da droben auf jenem berge)

London 18-19 February 1987	Johnson	CD: Hyperion CDJ 33001

schwestergruss (im mondenschein wall' ich auf und ab)

London August- December 1970	Moore	LP: EMI SLS 812/1C187 02172-02173 CD: EMI CZS 569 3892
Snape 14 June 1971	Leppard	CD: BBC Music Magazine BBCMM 143

schlummerlied (es mahnt der wald)

London August- December 1970	Moore	LP: EMI SLS 812/1C187 02172-02173 CD: EMI CZS 569 3892

sehnsucht (ach aus dieses tales gründen)

London 18-19 February 1987	Johnson	CD: Hyperion CDJ 33001

suleika-lieder: was bedeutet die bewegung?; ach um deine feuchten schwingen

London August- December 1970	Moore	LP: EMI SLS 812/1C187 02172-02173 CD: EMI CZS 569 3892 <u>Ach um deine feuchten Schwingen</u> LP: EMI SLS 5275

thekla (wo ich sei, und wo mich hingewendet)

London   Johnson   CD: Hyperion CDJ 33001
18-19
February
1987

der tod und das mädchen (vorüber, ach vorüber!)

London   Parsons   LP: EMI ASD 4054/1C063 43033
April-   CD: EMI CZS 569 3892
December
1980

die vögel (wie lieblich und fröhlich zu singen, zu schweben)

London   Moore   LP: EMI ASD 2431/1C063 00391
6-8   CD: EMI CDM 565 0092
November
1967

wanderers nachtlied (der du von dem himmel bist)

London   Johnson   CD: Hyperion CDJ 33001
18-19
February
1987

wiegenlieder: wie sich der äuglein kindischer himmel; schlafe, schlafe, holder süsser knabe

London August- December 1970	Moore	LP: EMI SLS 812/1C187 01272-02173 CD: EMI CZS 569 3892 <u>Schlafe, schlafe, holder süsser Knabe</u> LP: EMI SLS 5275

wonne der wehmut (trocknet nicht, tränen der ewigen liebe!)

London 18-19 February 1987	Johnson	CD: Hyperion CDJ 33001

zögernd leise/rosamunde

London 1973	ECO Chorus Leppard	LP: Philips 9500 307/6767 001

könnt' ich ewig hier/alfonso und estrella

London 1973	ECO Leppard	LP: Philips 9500 307/6767 001

so schlummert auf rosen/lazarus

London 1973	ECO Leppard	LP: Philips 9500 307/6767 001

<u>Many of the Schubert Lieder recorded in 1987 for Graham Johnson's complete edition are in the composer's second, or alternative, settings</u>

HEINRICH SCHUETZ (1585-1672)

duets: der herr schaut vom himmel; verbum caro factum est, allelulia

London February 1970	Fischer-Dieskau Instrumentalists	LP: EMI ASD 2710 LP: Angel 36712

ROBERT SCHUMANN (1810-1856)

frauenliebe und -leben, song cycle

London 1965	Isepp	LP: Saga XID 5277/STXID 5277 CD: Saga SCD 9001
London August 1968	Barenboim	EMI unpublished
London July 1975	Barenboim	LP: EMI ASD 3217/1C063 02704 CD: EMI CZS 568 6672

liederkreis op 39

London July 1975	Barenboim	LP: EMI ASD 3217/1C063 02704

duets: er und sie; wiegenlied; ich bin dein baum; schön ist das fest des lenzes; herbstlied; tanzlied

London 21-23 August 1969	Fischer-Dieskau Barenboim	LP: EMI ASD 2553/1C063 02041

CHARLES STANFORD (1852-1924)

la belle dame sans merci

London	Moore	LP: EMI HQS 1091/ESD 100 6421/SLS 5275
9-10		LP: Angel 36456
February		CD: EMI CDM 565 0092
1967		

ALESSANDRO STRADELLA (1644-1682)

ragion sempre addita

London	ASMIF	LP: Philips 9500 557
January	Marriner	CD: Philips 434 1732
1978		

RICHARD STRAUSS (1864-1949)

all mein gedanken

London 6-8 November 1967	Moore	LP: EMI ASD 2431/1C063 00391

allerseelen (stell' auf den tisch die duftenden reseden)

London 6-8 November 1967	Moore	LP: EMI ASD 2431/1C063 00391

befreit (du wirst nicht weinen)

London 6-8 November 1967	Moore	LP: EMI ASD 2431/1C063 00391 CD: EMI CDM 565 0092

heimliche aufforderung (auf, hebe die funkelnde schale!)

London 6-8 November 1967	Moore	LP: EMI ASD 2431/1C063 00391/SLS 5275

liebeshymnus (heil jenem tag!)

London 3-24 June 1975	LPO Boult	LP: EMI ASD 3260/1C065 02758 LP: Angel 32019/34454/37199 CD: EMI CDC 747 8542/CDM 767 8432

morgen (und morgen wird die sonne wieder scheinen)

London 6-8 November 1967	Moore	LP: EMI ASD 2431/SEOM 8/ 1C063 00391/SLS 5275 CD: EMI CDM 565 0092

muttertändelei (seht mir doch, mein schönes kind!)

London	LPO	LP: EMI ASD 3260/1C065 02758
3-24	Boult	LP: Angel 32019/34454/37199
June		CD: EMI CDC 747 8542/CDM 767 8432
1975		

die nacht (aus dem walde tritt die nacht)

London	Moore	LP: EMI ASD 2431/1C063 00391
6-8		
November		
1967		

das rosenband (im frühlingsschatten fand ich sie)

London	LPO	LP: EMI ASD 3260/1C065 02758
3-24	Boult	LP: Angel 32019/34454/37199
June		CD: EMI CDC 747 8542/CDM 767 8432
1975		

ruhe, meine seele

London	LPO	LP: EMI ASD 3260/1C065 02758
3-24	Boult	LP: Angel 32019/34454/37199
June		CD: EMI CDC 747 8542/CDM 767 8432
1975		

ständchen (mach auf! doch leise, mein kind!)

London	Moore	LP: EMI ASD 2929/1C063 02439
13-16		
October		
1972		

wiegenlied (träume, du mein süsses leben!)

London	Moore	LP: EMI ASD 2431/1C063 00391
6-8		
November		
1967		

ARTHUR SULLIVAN (1842-1900)

orpheus with his lute

London 13-16 October 1972	Moore	LP: EMI ASD 2929/1C063 02439

RANDALL THOMPSON (1899-1984)

the knight of bethlehem

Cambridge 30-31 October 1980	Ledger	LP: EMI ASD 3981

MICHAEL TIPPETT (1905-1997)

a child of our time

Wembley 21-23 March 1975	Norman, Cassilly, Shirley-Quirk BBC Choirs BBC SO Davis	LP: Philips 6500 985 CD: Philips 420 0752/446 3312

RALPH VAUGHAN WILLIAMS (1872-1958)

hodie, christmas cantata

London January- February 1965	Lewis, Shirley-Quirk Bach Choir LSO Willcocks	LP: Columbia 33SX 1782/SCX 3570 LP: Angel 36297 LP: EMI SLS 5082

the call

London 1962	Isepp	LP: Saga XIP 7013/XID 5213/STXID 5213 CD: Saga SCD 9012
Cambridge 30-31 October 1980	Ledger	LP: EMI ASD 3981

youth and love

London 1962	Isepp	LP: Saga XIP 7013/XID 5213/STXID 5213 CD: Saga SCD 9012

linden lea

London 9-10 February 1967	Moore	LP: EMI HQS 1091/ESD 100 6421 LP: Angel 36456 CD: EMI CDM 565 0092

GIUSEPPE VERDI (1813-1901)

requiem

Chicago 1-2 June 1977	L.Price, Luchetti, Van Dam Chicago SO and Chorus Solti	LP: Victor RL 02476/ARL2-2476 CD: RCA/BMG RD 82476/09026 614032

te deum/4 pezzi sacri

London 10-13 December 1962	Philharmonia Orchestra & Chorus Giulini	LP: EMI AN 120/SAN 120/SXLP 30508/ 1C053 00016 LP: Angel 36125 CD: EMI CDS 747 2578

ANTONIO VIVALDI (1678-1741)

gloria

London July 1966	Vaughan Kings College Choir ASMIF Willcocks	LP: Decca RG 505/ZRG 505 CD: Decca 425 7242

RICHARD WAGNER (1813-1883)

wesendonk-lieder

London 3 November 1971	BBC SO Goodall	Unpublished radio broadcast
London 3-24 June 1975	LPO Boult	LP: EMI ASD 3260/1C065 02758 LP: Angel 32019/34454/37199 CD: EMI CDC 747 8542/CDM 767 8432

WILLIAM WALTON (1902-1983)

troilus and cressida

London 12-30 November 1976	Role of Cressida Bainbridge, Cassilly, English, Luxon Covent Garden Orchestra & Chorus Foster	LP: EMI SLS 997 CD: EMI CMS 565 5502

PETER WARLOCK (1894-1930)

balulalow

London 1962	Isepp	LP: Saga XIP 7013/XID 5213/STXID 5213 CD: Saga SCD 9012
Cambridge 30-31 October 1980	Ledger	LP: EMI ASD 3981

youth

London 1962	Isepp	LP: Saga XIP 7013/XID 5213/STXID 5213 CD: Saga SCD 9012

pretty ring time

London 9-10 February 1967	Moore	LP: EMI HQS 1091/ESD 100 6421 LP: Angel 36465 CD: EMI CDM 565 0092

98 Baker

HUGO WOLF (1860-1903)

spanisches liederbuch: nun wandre, maria; die ihr schwebt um diese palmen; ach des knaben augen; herr, was trägt der boden hier?

London November 1967	Moore	LP: EMI ASD 2431/1C063 00391

<u>Die ihr schwebt & Was trägt der Boden</u>
LP: EMI SLS 5275

MISCELLANEOUS

were you there when they crucified my lord, negro spiritual

Cambridge 30-31 October 1980	Ledger	LP: EMI ASD 3981

comin' thro the rye, scottish folksong

London December 1968	Moore	LP: EMI 1C147 30636-30637

Margarete Klose
1902-1968

JOHANN SEBASTIAN BACH (1685-1750)

matthäus-passion

Leipzig 19 April 1935	Feuge, Pataky, Schöffler, Böhme Leipzig SO and Choirs Weisbach	LP: Acanta FA 23076 CD: Preiser 90099

JULIUS BITTNER

das höllische gold, excerpt (wohin? ins haus!)

Berlin December 1932	Erhard Berlin RO E.Kleiber	LP: Acanta 22.21776/98.21776

GEORGES BIZET (1838-1875)

carmen, excerpt (l'amour est un oiseau rebelle)

Berlin 1941	Städtische Oper Orchestra Steeger <u>Sung in German</u>	78: Grammophon 67789 CD: Preiser 89082

carmen, excerpt (près des remparts de séville)

Berlin 1941	Städtische Oper Orchestra Steeger <u>Sung in German</u>	78: Grammophon 62862 LP: Historia H 667-668 CD: Preiser 89082 <u>Historia incorrectly dated 1942</u>

carmen, excerpt (en vain pour éviter)

Berlin 1941	Städtische Oper Orchestra Steeger <u>Sung in German</u>	78: Grammophon 67789 LP: Historia H 667-668 CD: Preiser 89082
Berlin 1942	Staatskapelle Heger <u>Sung in German</u>	LP: Acanta 22.21484

carmen, excerpt (vive escamillo!/si tu m'aimes/c'est toi! c'est moi!)

Berlin December 1932	Gerson, Fischer, Wittrisch, Staatskapelle and Chorus Zweig <u>Sung in German</u>	78: HMV DB 4418 LP: Electrola E 83381 LP: EMI 1C147 29128-29129 LP: Historia H 667-668 CD: Preiser 89082/89989 <u>Historia incorrectly dated 1933</u>

JOHANNES BRAHMS (1833-1897)

die mainacht (wann der silberne mond durch die gesträuche blinkt)

Berlin   Raucheisen   LP: Historia H 667-668
1942

heimweh II (o wüsst' ich doch den weg züruck)

Berlin   Wetzel   78: Clangor MD 9603
1935   LP: Historia H 667-668

ANTONIN DVORAK (1841-1904)

moravian duets

Berlin   Fuchs   LP: Melodiya M10 47335 000
1943-1944   Raucheisen
                Sung in German

FRIEDRICH VON FLOTOW (1812-1883)

martha, excerpt (mag der himmel euch vergeben)

Berlin   Berger,   78: HMV DB 4411
1934   Wittrisch,   LP: Electrola E 83381
                Domgraf-Fassbänder
                Staatskapelle
                and Chorus
                Kuhn

TOMMASO GIORDANI (1733-1806)

caro mio ben

Berlin 1932	Orchestra	78: Electrola EH 993
Munich 4-5 January 1955	Munich PO Leitner	45: DG NL 32 027

MIKHAIL GLINKA (1804-1857)

ruslan and lyudmila, excerpt (o my ratmir!)

Berlin 1943	Berlin RO Rother Sung in German	LP: Eterna 820 922

EDVARD GRIEG (1843-1907)

songs: herbststurm; unter rosen; eros; weihnachtswiegenlied; der jäger; stelldichein

Berlin 21 May 1943	Raucheisen	LP: Acanta 40.23559

CHRISTOPH WILLIBALD GLUCK (1714-1787)

orfeo ed euridice

Berlin 2 March 1952	Role of Orfeo Berger, Streich Städtische Oper Orchestra & Chorus Rother	LP: Urania URLP 223/URLP 5223-3 LP: Acanta FA 22140/30.22140/ DE 21804 Excerpts LP: Urania UR 8015/US 59

orfeo ed euridice, excerpt (che puro ciel!)

Munich 15-16 November 1955	Munich PO Rother Sung in German	45: DG 30 255 LP: DG LPE 17 066/LPEM 19 053/ 478 128/89 538 LP: Heliodor (USA) H 25005/HS 25005

orfeo ed euridice, excerpt (che farò)

Berlin 1938	Staatskapelle Seidler-Winkler Sung in German	78: Electrola DB 4531 CD: Preiser 89082
Berlin 1942	Staatskapelle Rother Sung in German	LP: Acanta 22.21484
Berlin 1943	Staatskapelle Heger Sung in German	LP: Eterna 820 922
Berlin 21 September 1944	BPO Abendroth Sung in German	CD: Tahra TAH 192-193
Berlin 8 April 1954	Berlin RO Rother Sung in German	78: DG LV 36 113 45: DG NL 32 053 LP: LPE 17 066/LPEM 19 053/ 478 128/89 538 LP: Heliodor (USA) H 25005/HS 25005
Berlin 8 April 1954	Berlin RO Rother	78: DG LV 36 114 45: DG NL 32 054

WAGNER
(1813–1883)

DIE WALKÜRE

THE CAST

Brünnhilde, *Soprano*	MARTHA MÖDL
Siegmund, *Tenor*	LUDWIG SUTHAUS
Sieglinde, *Soprano*	LEONIE RYSANEK
Wotan, *Baritone*	FERDINAND FRANTZ
Hunding, *Bass*	GOTTLOB FRICK
Fricka, *Soprano*	MARGARETE KLOSE

Valkyries

Gerhilde, *Soprano*	GERDA SCHREYER
Ortlinde, *Soprano*	JUDITH HELLWIG
Waltraute, *Soprano*	DAGMAR SCHMEDES
Schwertleite, *Contralto*	RUTH SIEWERT
Helmwige, *Soprano*	ERIKA KÖTH
Siegrune, *Contralto*	HERTHA TÖPPER
Grimgerde, *Contralto*	JOHANNA BLATTER
Rossweisse, *Contralto*	DAGMAR HERMANN

VIENNA PHILHARMONIC ORCHESTRA
Conductor: WILHELM FURTWÄNGLER

Recorded in the Musikvereinsaal, Vienna

"HIS MASTER'S VOICE"

LONG  PLAY

33⅓ R.P.M RECORDS

Record Nos. ALP 1257-61   Record Library Series LP No. 630

Distributing Organisation for Great Britain:
THE GRAMOPHONE COMPANY LIMITED
RECORD DIVISION, 8-11, GREAT CASTLE STREET, LONDON, W.1

Export Distributing Organisation:
E.M.I. INTERNATIONAL LIMITED, HAYES, MIDDLESEX, ENGLAND

BÜHNENFESTSPIELE BAYREUTH

MONTAG, DEN 14. AUGUST 1939

TRISTAN UND ISOLDE

Musikalische Leitung: Victor de Sabata

Inszenierung: Heinz Tietjen

Bühnenbild und Trachten: Emil Preetorius

Chöre: Friedrich Jung

Isolde	Germaine Lubin
Tristan	Karl Buschmann
Marke	Josef v. Manowarda
Kurwenal	Jaro Prohaska
Brangäne	Margarete Klose
Hirt	Gustav Rödin
Melot	Fritz Wolff
Junger Seemann	Benno Arnold
Steuermann	Edwin Heyer

1. Akt: Zur See auf dem Verdeck von Tristans Schiff während der Überfahrt von Irland nach Kornwall
2. Akt: In der Königlichen Burg Markes in Kornwall / 3. Akt: Tristans Burg in Bretagne

Technische Leitung und Beleuchtung: Paul Eberhardt · Kostümwesen: Kurt Palm

Beginn: 1. Aufzug 16 Uhr   2. Aufzug: 18.15 Uhr   3. Aufzug: 20.30 Uhr

orfeo ed euridice (chiamo il mio ben!)

Berlin 1938	Staatskapelle Seidler-Winkler <u>Sung in German</u>	78: Electrola DB 4531 CD: Preiser 89082
Berlin 9 April 1954	Berlin RO Rother <u>Sung in German</u>	78: DG LV 36 113 45: DG NL 32 053 LP: DG LPE 17 066/LPEM 19 053/ 478 128/89 538 LP: Heliodor (USA) H 25005/HS 25005
Berlin 9 April 1954	Berlin RO Rother	78: DG LV 36 114 45: DG NL 32 054

alceste, excerpt (divinités du styx!)

Berlin 1938	Staatskapelle Seidler-Winkler <u>Sung in German</u>	78: Electrola DB 4532 LP: Electrola E 83381 LP: Historia H 667-668 LP: Preiser LV 18 CD: Preiser 99082

paride ed elena, excerpt (o del mio dolce ardor)

Berlin 1938	Staatskapelle Seidler-Winkler <u>Sung in German</u>	78: Electrola DB 4532 LP: Preiser LV 18 CD: Preiser 89082

GEORGE FRIDERIC HANDEL (1685-1759)

giulio cesare, excerpt (v'adoro pupille)

Berlin 21 September 1944	BPO Abendroth Sung in German	LP: Eterna 820 922 LP: Acanta 98.221776 CD: Tahra TAH 192-193 Acanta incorrectly dated 1947
Munich 15 November 1955	Bamberg SO Rother Sung in German	45: DG EPL 30 255 LP: DG LPE 17 066

serse, excerpt (ombra mai fù)

Berlin 1932	Orchestra	78: Electrola EH 993/EH 1284
Berlin 1941	Berlin RO Heger Sung in German	LP: Acanta 22.21484 LP: Historia H 667-668 Historia incorrectly dated 1934
Munich 4-5 January 1955	Munich PO Leitner	45: DG NL 32 027 LP: DG LPE 17 066

CLAUDIO MONTEVERDI (1567-1643)

l'arianna, excerpt (lasciatemi morir, arranged by orff)

Berlin 30 October 1943	Staatskapelle Heger Sung in German	LP: Eterna 820 922 LP: Acanta 22.21484

110 Klose

WOLFGANG AMADEUS MOZART (1756-1791)

die zauberflöte

Berlin
June
1955
	Role of 3rd Lady
	Stader, Streich,
	Otto, Haefliger,
	Fischer-Dieskau,
	Greindl, Borg
	RIAS Choir
	Berlin RO
	Fricsay
		LP: DG LPM 18 264-18 266/
		    LPM 18 267-18 269/89 662-89 664/
		    2701 003/2728 009/2730 014
		CD: DG 435 7412
		Excerpts
		45: DG EPL 30 237
		LP: DG LPEM 19 194/89 653
		LP: Decca (USA) DL 9932

OTTO NICOLAI (1810-1849)

die lustigen weiber von windsor, excerpt (das ist wirklich doch zu keck!)

Munich 17 May 1955	Stader Munich PO Leitner	LP: DG LPEM 19 049/89 648

JACQUES OFFENBACH (1819-1880)

les contes d'hoffmann

Berlin 29 July 1946	Role of Antonia's Mother Berger, Streich, Klein, Anders, Prohaska Berlin RO and Chorus Rother Sung in German	LP: Urania URLP 224 LP: Royale 1269-1271 LP: Gramophone (USA) 20154-20156 LP: Acanta DE 21804/22.21804/40.21804

les contes d'hoffmann, excerpt (je l'ai promis, je ne chanterais plus!)

Berlin 1-5 November 1954	Streich, Metternich Berlin SO Schüchter Sung in German	45: Electrola E 50088 LP: Electrola E 60061/E 83381 LP: EMI 1C047 28181/1C047 28577

HANS PFITZNER (1869-1949)

palestrina, excerpt (allein in dunkler tiefe)

Berlin 20 September 1949	Schlemm, Streich, Trötschel, Fehenberger Komische Oper Orchestra Heger	78: DG LM 68 420 45: DG NL 32 204

GIACOMO PUCCINI (1858-1924)

madama butterfly, excerpt (scuoti quella fronda)

Berlin 1937	Perras Staatskapelle Seidler-Winkler Sung in German	45: Electrola DB 4501 LP: Electrola E 83381

CAMILLE SAINT-SAENS (1835-1921)

samson et dalila, excerpt (mon coeur s'ouvre à ta voix)

Berlin 1932	Staatskapelle Schmidt Sung in German	78: Clangor MD 9673 LP: Electrola E 83381 LP: Historia H 667-668 CD: Preiser 89082 Historia incorrectly dated 1935
Berlin 1937	Staatskapelle Rother Sung in German	LP: Acanta 22.21484
Berlin 20 January 1946	BPO Celibidache Sung in German	LP: Eterna 820 922 CD: Tahra TAH 273 Group of Wolf orchestral songs also performed at this concert

FRANZ SCHUBERT (1797-1828)

Du bist die Ruh

Berlin   Wetzel   78: Clangor MD 9601
1935

fragment aus dem aischylos (so wird der mann, der sonder zwang gerecht ist)

Berlin   Raucheisen   Unpublished radio broadcast
1944

der geistertanz (die bretterne kammer der toten erbebt)

Berlin   Raucheisen   CD: Preiser 89231
1944

gretchen am spinnrade (meine ruh' ist hin, mein herz ist schwer)

Berlin   Raucheisen   LP: Historia H 667-668
1942

iphigenia (blüht denn hier an tauris strande)

Berlin   Raucheisen   Unpublished radio broadcast
1944

die junge nonne (wie braust durch die wipfel der heulende sturm)

Berlin   Raucheisen   Unpublished radio broadcast
1944

der könig in thule (es war ein könig in thule)

Berlin   Raucheisen   Unpublished radio broadcast
1944

nachtgesang (tiefe feier schauert um die welt)

Berlin   Raucheisen   Unpublished radio broadcast
1944

der tod und das mädchen (vorüber, ach vorüber!)

Berlin   Wetzel   78: Clangor MD 9601
1935   LP: Historia H 667-668

verklärung (lebensfunke, vom himmel entglüht)

Berlin   Raucheisen   Unpublished radio broadcast
1944

ROBERT SCHUMANN (1810-1856)

frühlingsnacht/liederkreis

Berlin   Raucheisen   LP: Saga 7007
1944

die kartenlegerin (schlief die mutter endlich ein)

Berlin   Raucheisen   LP: Saga 7007
1944

lust der sturmnacht (wenn durch berg und tale draussen)

Berlin   Raucheisen   LP: Saga 7007
1944

talismane/myrthen

Berlin   Raucheisen   Unpublished radio broadcast
1944

waldesgespräch/liederkreis

Berlin   Wetzel   78: Clangor MD 9603
1935   LP: Historia H 667-668

RICHARD STRAUSS (1864-1949)

elektra

Frankfurt 31 January 1953	<u>Role of Klytemnestra</u> Borkh, Kupper, Bensing, Frantz Hessischer Rundfunk Orchestra & Chorus Schröder	CD: Melodram GM 30007

salome

Frankfurt 9 May 1952	<u>Role of Herodias</u> Borkh, Lorenz, Fehringer, Frantz Hessischer Rundfunk Orchestra Schröder	CD: Myto MCD 93592
Munich 21-25 June 1953	Varnay, Hopf, Patzak, Braun Bavarian RO Weigert	LP: Estro armonico EA 035 LP: Discocorp IGI 289 CD: Bella voce 107.210

befreit (du wirst nicht weinen)

Berlin   Raucheisen   78: Grammophon LM 68 124
1942

geduld (geduld, sagst du, und zeigst mit weissem finger)

Berlin   Raucheisen   LP: Acanta 40.23546
28 November   CD: Bella voce 107.210
1944

in gold'ner fülle (wir schreiten in gold'ner fülle)

Berlin   Raucheisen   78: Grammophon LM 68 124
1942   LP: Historia H 667-668

die nacht (aus dem walde tritt die nacht)

Berlin   Wetzel   78: Clangor MD 9605
1936   LP: Historia H 667-668

traum durch die dämmerung (weite wiesen im dämmergrau)

Berlin   Wetzel   78: Clangor MD 9605
1936   LP: Historia H 667-668

PIOTR TCHAIKOVSKY (1840-1893)

pique dame

Berlin 1946-1947	<u>Role of Countess</u> Grümmer, Schock, Nissen, Prohaska Städtische Oper Chorus Berlin RO Rother <u>Sung in German</u>	LP: Urania URLP 207 LP: Classics Club X 135-136 <u>Abridged recording</u>

118   Klose

GIUSEPPE VERDI (1813-1901)

requiem

Salzburg 14 August 1949	Zadek, Rosvaenge, Christoff Wiener Singverein VPO Karajan	LP: Cetra LO 524 LP: Discocorp RR 361 LP: Rodolphe RP 12403-12404 LP: Dei della musica DMV 34-35 CD: Datum DAT 12323

aida

Frankfurt 1952	<u>Role of Amneris</u> Kupper, Lorenz, Gonzsar Hessischer Rundfunk Orchestra & Chorus Schröder <u>Sung in German</u>	CD: Myto MCD 962146

aida, excerpt (fu la sortè dell' armi!)

Berlin 1937	Perras Staatskapelle Seidler-Winkler <u>Sung in German</u>	78: Electrola DB 4500-4501 LP: Historia H 667-668 CD: Preiser 89082 <u>Historia incorrectly dated 1936</u>

aida, excerpt (ohimè! morir mi sento!)

Berlin 1942	Schirp Berlin RO Rother <u>Sung in German</u>	LP: Acanta BB 22025

aida, excerpt (o terra addio!)

Berlin 1934	Teschemacher, Wittrisch Orchestra <u>Sung in German</u>	78: Electrola DB 4409

un ballo in maschera, excerpt (rè dell' abisso!)

Berlin 1936	Staatskapelle Seidler-Winkler <u>Sung in German</u>	78: Electrola DB 4461 LP: Historia H 667-668 LP: Preiser LV 18 CD: Preiser 89082 <u>Historia incorrectly dated 1935</u>

don carlo, excerpt (o don fatale)

Berlin 1936	Staatskapelle Seidler-Winkler <u>Sung in German</u>	78: Electrola DB 4461 LP: Electrola E 83381 LP: Historia H 667-668 LP: Preiser LV 18 CD: Preiser 89082 <u>Historia incorrectly dated 1935</u>
Berlin 24 June 1942	Berlin RO Rother <u>Sung in German</u>	LP: Acanta BB 22318/22.21484 CD: Preiser 90257 CD: Hamburger Archiv für Gesangskunst HAGLEM 2

don carlo, excerpt (giustizia o sire!)

Berlin 24 June 1942	Lemnitz, Hann, Ahlersmeyer Berlin RO Rother <u>Sung in German</u>	LP: Acanta BB 22318/22.22110/22.21484 CD: Preiser 90257 CD: Hamburger Archiv für Gesangskunst HAGLEM 2 <u>Recording continues directly into the</u> <u>version of O don fatale listed above</u>

rigoletto

Berlin 20-22 November 1944	Role of Maddalena Berger, Rosvaenge, Schlusnus, Greindl Staatskapelle and Chorus Heger Sung in German	LP: Urania URLP 222 LP: DG LPEM 19 222-19 223/88 026-88 027 LP: Eterna 820 152-820 153 CD: Preiser 90036 Excerpts LP: Acanta 22.21484
Berlin 20-23 September 1950	Streich, Schock, Metternich, Hoppe Berlin Radio Orchestra & Chorus Fricsay Sung in German	CD: Myto MCD 945111

rigoletto, excerpt (bella figlia dell' amore)

Berlin 1934	Berger, Wittrisch, Domgraf-Fassbänder Städtische Oper Orchestra Zweig Sung in German	78: Electrola DB 4414 LP: Electrola E 83381 LP: Preiser LV 120 CD: Preiser 89082

il trovatore, excerpt (stride la vampa)

Berlin 1937	Staatskapelle Seidler-Winkler Sung in German	78: Electrola DB 4502 LP: Historia H 667-668 LP: Preiser LV 18 CD: Preiser 89082 Historia incorrectly dated 1936
Berlin 1944	Staatskapelle Heger Sung in German	LP: Acanta 22.21484

il trovatore, excerpt (condotta all' era in ceppi)

Berlin 1937	Staatskapelle Seidler-Winkler Sung in German	78: Electrola DB 4502 LP: Historia H 667-668 LP: Preiser LV 18 CD: Preiser 89082 Historia incorrectly dated 1936
Berlin 1944	Staatskapelle Heger Sung in German	LP: Acanta 22.21484

il trovatore, excerpt (ai nostri monti)

Berlin December 1932	Wittrisch Staatskapelle Zweig Sung in German	78: Electrola DA 4407 LP: EMI 1C147 29128-29129M LP: Historia H 663-664/H 667-668 CD: Preiser 89082 Historia incorrectly dated 1933

RICHARD WAGNER (1813-1883)

götterdämmerung

Rome 20-27 November 1953	<u>Roles of Waltraute and First Norn</u> Mödl, Jurinac, Suthaus, Poell, Pernerstorfer, Greindl RAI Roma Orchestra & Chorus Furtwängler	LP: MRF Records MRF 34 LP: EMI RLS 702/EX 29 06703/ 1C147 02288-02292M LP: Angel 6079 CD: Arkadia CDWFE 359 CD: EMI CZS 767 1362/CZS 767 1232

götterdämmerung, excerpt (frau sonne sendet lichte strahlen)

Berlin 7 November 1944	Langhammer, Scheppan, Lorenz Staatskapelle Heger	LP: Acanta 22.21484/22.22120/40.23502 CD: Myto MCD 93592 CD: Preiser 90245 <u>Myto and Preiser issues contain entire Act 3 up to and including Trauermarsch</u>

lohengrin

Berlin 1942	<u>Role of Ortrud</u> Müller, Völker, Prohaska, Hofmann, Grossmann Staatskapelle and Chorus Heger	LP: Preiser LOH 2B CD: Preiser 90043 Excerpts LP: Acanta 22.21484/40.23502/98.22177 LP: Historia H 667-668
Munich 22 December 1949	Schech, Vincent, A.Böhm, Böhme, Wolff Bavarian State Orchestra & Chorus Kempe	LP: Urania URLP 225 LP: Nixa ULP 9225 LP: Acanta HB 22326/40.22326 CD: Pilz 44.21182/44.21332 Excerpts LP: Urania UR 7123
Hamburg 6-11 July 1953	Cunitz, Schock, Metternich, Frick, Günter NDR Orchestra and Chorus Schüchter	LP: HMV ALP 1095-1098 LP: Electrola E 90061-90064 LP: Victor LHMV 1095-1098 CD: EMI CHS 565 5172 Excerpts LP: Electrola E 83381

lohengrin, excerpt (mein herr und gott)

Bayreuth 24 August 1936	Müller, Völker, Prohaska, Manowarda Bayreuth Festival Orchestra & Chorus Tietjen	78: Telefunken SKB 2050/SKB 02050 LP: Telefunken KT 11017 LP: EMI 1C181 30669-30678M CD: Teldec 9031 764422

lohengrin, excerpt (durch gottes sieg ist jetzt dein leben mein!)

Vienna 19 June 1938	Müller, Völker, Prohaska, Manowarda, Grossmann Vienna Opera Chorus VPO Tietjen	CD: Koch 3-1468-2 <u>Guest performance by Berlin Staatsoper</u>

lohengrin, excerpt (elsa! ist meine stimme dir so fremd?/entweihte götter!)

Vienna 19 June 1938	Müller, Völker, Prohaska, Manowarda, Grossmann Vienna Opera Chorus VPO Tietjen	CD: Koch 3-1468-2 <u>Guest performance by Berlin Staatsoper</u>
Berlin 1942	Lemnitz, Prohaska Staatskapelle Schüler	CD: Hamburger Archiv für Gesangskunst HAGLEM 3
Berlin 30 January 1948	Lemnitz Staatskapelle Schüler	LP: World Records SHB 47 LP: Preiser LV 101/LV 160 LP: EMI 1C147 28989-28990M/EX 29 02123 CD: Preiser 89167 CD: Voce della luna VL 20002 Entweihte Götter only LP: EMI 1C181 30669-30678M

<u>All recordings of the above scene commence with Elsa's Euch Lüften; Vienna</u>
<u>performance also continues with Ortrud's Nicht länger will ich dulden until</u>
<u>the end of Act 2</u>

lohengrin, excerpt (mein lieber schwan....to end of opera)

Bayreuth 19 July 1936	Müller, Völker, Manowarda Bayreuth Festival Orchestra & Chorus Furtwängler	LP: Ed Smith EJS 399 LP: French Furtwängler Society SWF 7801 LP: Cetra FE 25 LP: Acanta 40.23520 CD: Fonoteam CD 74807 CD: Acanta 44.1055 <u>Acanta CD incorrectly dated 1931</u>

das rheingold, excerpt (weiche, wotan, weiche!)

1929	Weber Orchestra Hoesslin	78: Pathé X 7197 LP: EMI 1C181 30669-30678M
Berlin 9 April 1954	BPO Rother	78: DG L 62 935 45: DG NL 32 026 LP: DG LPE 17 066

rienzi, excerpt (gerechter gott! so ist's entschieden schon!)

Berlin 1942	Berlin RO Rother	LP: Acanta 22.21484/40.23502/DE 23035 LP: Historia H 667-668 LP: Eterna 820 922 CD: Preiser 90223 <u>40.23502 states conductor to be Heger</u>

rienzi, excerpts (erstehe, hohe roma, neu!; rienzi, gib mir meinen vater!; verlässt die kirche mich....to end of opera)

Berlin 1941	Scheppan, Lorenz, Prohaska, Rödin, Hiller, Linde Staatskapelle and Chorus Schüler	LP: Acanta DE 23035/22.21484/40.23502 CD: Preiser 90223 <u>Erstehe hohe Roma neu</u> CD: Preiser 90213

rienzi, unspecified scenes

Leipzig 13 November 1937	Dobay, Seider, Gonszar Leipzig SO and Chorus Weisbach	Unpublished radio broadcast

siegfried

Rome 10-17 November 1953	Role of Erda Mödl, Streich, Suthaus, Patzak, Pernerstorfer, Frantz, Greindl RAI Roma Orchestra Furtwängler	LP: MRF Records MRF 23 LP: EMI RLS 702/EX 29 06703/ 1C147 02283-02288M LP: Angel 6078 CD: EMI CZS 767 1312/CZS 767 1232 CD: Arkadia CDWFE 359

tristan und isolde

Berlin 14-19 May 1943	Role of Brangäne Buchner, Lorenz, Hofmann, Prohaska Staatskapelle and Chorus Heger	LP: Acanta DE 22316 CD: Preiser 90243 Excerpts LP: Acanta 22.21484/40.23502/98.22177 LP: Eterna 821 028/821 029 LP: Historia H 667-668
Vienna 2 January 1943	A.Konetzni, Lorenz, Alsen, Schöffler Vienna Opera Chorus VPO Furtwängler	CD: Koch 3-1461-2 Acts 1 and 2 incomplete
Hamburg 16 December 1949	Baumann, Lorenz T.Herrmann, Kronenberg NDR Orchestra and Chorus Schmidt-Isserstedt	LP: Melodram CD: Myto MCD 981178
Munich 23 July 1950	Braun, Treptow, Frantz, Schöffler Bavarian State Orchestra & Chorus Knappertsbusch	LP: Discocorp LP: Movimento musica 05.001 CD: Laudis LCD 44009 CD: Gala GL 100.651 CD: Orfeo C356 943
Munich 29 July 1952	Braun, Treptow, Frantz, Grossmann Bavarian State Orchestra & Chorus E.Kleiber	LP: Melodram MEL 014

tristan und isolde, acts 1 and 2

London 18 June 1937	Role of Brangäne Flagstad, Melchior, Janssen, Nilssen Covent Garden Chorus LPO Beecham	LP: Anna Records ANNA 1059 Act 1 LP: Ed Smith UORC 302 LP: Discocorp RR 223 Act 2 LP: Discocorp RR 223 CD: EMI CHS 764 0372 <u>Initial release of CHS 764 0372</u> <u>incorrectly stated that entire recording</u> <u>was conducted by Beecham, whereas the</u> <u>parts not specified above were from a</u> <u>1936 performanced conducted by Reiner</u> <u>and with Kalter as Brangäne</u>

tristan und isolde, acts 2 and 3

Berlin
3 October
1947
	Schlüter, Suthaus,
	Prohaska, Frick
	Staatskapelle
	and Chorus
	Furtwängler
		LP: French Furtwängler Society
		    SWF 8205-8207
		LP: Cetra FE 43
		CD: Cetra CDE 1046
		CD: French Furtwängler Society
		    awaiting publication
		Excerpts
		LP: Cetra FE 25
		LP: Acanta 40.23520
		CD: Acanta 43.121/44.1055
		CD: Fonoteam CD 74807
		<u>All editions have standard cut in</u>
		<u>Act 2 Liebesnacht</u>

tristan und isolde, excerpt (einsam wachend)

Vienna 25 December 1941	A.Konetzni, Lorenz VPO Furtwängler	LP: Ed Smith EJS 399/UORC 267 LP: Acanta HB 22863 CD: Koch 3-1456-2
Berlin 9 April 1954	BPO Rother	78: DG L 62 935 45: DG NL 32 026 LP: DG LPE 17 066/LPEM 19 018/2721 115 LP: Decca (USA) DL 9897

tristan und isolde, excerpt (hörst du sie noch?/frau minne kenntest du nicht?)

Vienna 25 December 1941	A.Konetzni VPO Furtwängler	CD: Koch 3-1461-2

die walküre

Berlin 10 June 1951	<u>Role of Fricka</u> Buchner, Müller, Suthaus, Herrmann, Greindl Städtische Oper Orchestra Fricsay	CD: Myto MCD 93381
Vienna 28 September- 6 October 1954	Mödl, Rysanek, Suthaus, Frantz, Frick VPO Furtwängler	LP: HMV ALP 1257-1261/HQM 1019-1023 LP: Victor LHMV 900 LP: Electrola E 90100-90104/ WALP 1257-1261/SME 90100-90104 LP: HMV (France) FALP 383-387 LP: HMV (Italy) QALP 10098-10102 LP: Angel 6012 CD: EMI CHS 763 0452

die walküre, act 2 scene 1

Berlin 19-20 September 1938	Fuchs, Hotter Staatskapelle Seidler-Winkler	78: Electrola DB 3719-3721 LP: Electrola E 80686-80688 LP: EMI 29 02123 LP: Danacord CD: Danacord DACOCD 317-318 CD: EMI CDH 764 2552 <u>So ist es denn aus</u> 78: Electrola DB 4600 LP: Historia H 667-668 CD: Preiser 89082 <u>This recording formed part of a complete</u> <u>Act 2, some sections of which had been</u> <u>recorded in 1935 in Vienna to complement</u> Bruno Walter's version of Act 1 of the music drama

Montag, den 6. Dezember 1954
Allgemeiner Kartenverkauf und letzte Vorstellung im Abonnement XIV. Gruppe

DIE WALKÜRE

MUSIKDRAMA IN DREI AUFZÜGEN VON
RICHARD WAGNER

Musikalische Leitung: WILHELM LOIBNER

Inszenierung: ERICH WYMETAL

Siegmund	Günther Treptow
Hunding	Deszö Ernster
Wotan	Karl Kamann
Sieglinde	Hilde Konetzni
Brünnhilde	Gertrude Grob-Prandl
Fricka	Margarete Klose
Helmwige	Judith Hellwig
Gerhilde	Gerda Scheyrer
Ortlinde	Esther Réthy
Waltraute · Walküren	Mira Kalin
Siegrune	Maria Schober
Roßweiße	Dagmar Hermann
Grimgerde	Marta Rohs
Schwertleite	Polly Batic

Schauplatz der Handlung:

Erster Aufzug: Das Innere der Wohnung Hundings

Zweiter Aufzug: Wildes Felsengebirge

Dritter Aufzug: Auf dem Gipfel eines Felsenberges (des „Brünn-
hildensteines")

Nach jedem Aufzug eine größere Pause

Anfang 18 Uhr   Ende etwa 22½ Uhr

Kathleen Ferrier
1912-1953

JOHANN SEBASTIAN BACH (1685-1750)

mass in b minor

Vienna 15 June 1950	Schwarzkopf, W.Ludwig, Poell, Schöffler Wiener Singverein VSO Karajan	CD: Foyer 2CF-2022 CD: Arkadia CDKAR 212 CD: Verona 27073-27074 Excerpts CD: Verona 27076
London 17 July 1951	Danco, Pears, Boyce, Walker BBC Chorus Boyd Neel Orchestra Enesco	Unpublished radio broadcast Includes Ferrier's only recorded performance of the aria, Laudamus te

mass in b minor, excerpt (agnus dei)

Vienna 13-14 June 1950	VSO Karajan	CD: EMI CHS 769 7412 Recording incomplete
London 7 October 1952	LPO Boult	45: Decca 45-71138/CEP 722 LP: Decca LW 5038/LXT 2757/ LXT 5382/414 6231 LP: London LD 9096/LLP 688/5083 CD: Decca 414 6232/433 4742/433 8022 CD: Gala GL 307 Other LP reissues with stereo re-recording of orchestral accompaniment on Decca SXL 2234/SDD 286/AKF 1-7/SPA 322/SPA 531

mass in b minor, excerpt (christe eleison)

Vienna 13-14 June 1950	Schwarzkopf VSO Karajan	CD: EMI CDM 763 6552/CMS 763 7902

mass in b minor, excerpt (et in unum dominum)

Vienna 13-14 June 1950	Schwarzkopf VSO Karajan	CD: EMI CDM 763 6552/CMS 763 7902

mass in b minor, excerpt (qui sedes)

Vienna 13-14 June 1950	VSO Karajan	CD: EMI CHS 769 7412 Recording incomplete
London 7 October 1952	LPO Boult	45: Decca 45-71138/CEP 722 LP: Decca LW 5038/LXT 2757/ LXT 5382/414 6231 LP: London LD 9096/LLP 688/5083 CD: Decca 414 6232/433 4742/433 8022 Other LP reissues with stereo re-recording of orchestral accompaniment on Decca SXL 2234/SDD 286/AKF 1-7/SPA 531

saint matthew passion

London 30 June 1947- 11 June 1948	Suddaby, Greene, Parsons, Boyce, Clinton, Cummings Bach Choir Jacques Orchestra Jacques Sung in English	Abridged performance 78: Decca AK 2001-2021 LP: Decca ACL 109-111/D42 D3 LP: London A 43001 Excerpts 78: Decca K 1673-1679 CD: Decca 433 4692/433 8022
Vienna 9 June 1950	Seefried, W.Ludwig, Wiener, Schöffler, Edelmann, Berry Wiener Singverein VSO Karajan	LP: Foyer FO 1046 CD: Foyer 3CF-3013 CD: Arkadia CDKAR 211 CD: Verona 27070-27072 Excerpts CD: Verona 27076

saint matthew passion, excerpt (erbarme dich)

London 6 February 1946	National SO Sargent Sung in English	78: Decca K 1465 45: Decca 45-71037 LP: Decca LXT 6934/417 4661 CD: Decca 430 0962/433 4702/ 433 8022/458 8702 CD: Memoir CDMOIR 440

saint matthew passion, excerpt (buss und reu')

London 7 October 1952	LPO Boult	45: Decca CEP 721 LP: Decca LW 5083/LXT 2757/ LXT 5382/414 6231 LP: London LD 9096/LLP 688/5083 CD: Decca 414 6232/433 4742/433 8022 CD: Gala GL 307 Other LP reissues with stereo re-recording of orchestral accompaniment on Decca SXL 2234/SDD 286/AKF 1-7/SPA 531

saint john passion, excerpt (es ist vollbracht)

London 7 October 1952	LPO Boult	45: Decca 45-71112/CEP 721 LP: Decca LW 5038/LXT 2757/ LXT 5382/414 6231 LP: London LD 9096/LLP 688/5083 CD: Decca 414 6232/433 4742/433 8022 Other LP reissues with stereo re-recording of orchestral accompaniment on Decca SXL 2234/SDD 286/AKF 1-7/SPA 531

cantata no 11 "lobet gott in seinen reichen"

London
1 November
1949
	Mitchell,
	Herbert, Parsons
	Cantata Singers
	Jacques
	Orchestra
	Jacques
	Sung in English
		First version for 78s
		78: Decca AX 399-401
		Second version for LP
		LP: Decca LX 3006/ACL 52/
		    ECS 562/417 4661
		LP: London LPS 160/LLP 845/
		    5092/R 23206
		Excerpts
		LP: Decca LXT 6934
		CD: Decca 433 4702/433 8022

cantata no 67 "halt im gedächtnis jesum christ"

London 3 November 1949	Herbert, Parsons Cantata Singers Jacques Orchestra Jacques Sung in English	First version for 78s 78: Decca AX 347-348 Second version for LP LP: Decca LX 3007/ACL 52/ECS 563 LP: London LPS 161/5092/R 23206

ach dass nicht die letzte stunde/geistliche lieder und arien

London 15 December 1949	Silver, harpsichord	LP: Decca 414 0951 CD: Decca 433 4732/433 8022

bist du bei mir/anna magdalena notenbuch

New York January- March 1950	Newmark	CD: Decca 433 4732/433 8022/458 8702 <u>Voice of America broadcast</u>

vergiss mein nicht/geistliche lieder und arien

London 15 December 1949	Silver, harpsichord	LP: Decca 414 0951 CD: Decca 433 4732/433 8022

LUDWIG VAN BEETHOVEN (1770-1827)

symphony no 9 "choral"

London 13 November 1947	Baillie, Nash, Parsons LPO Choir LPO Walter	LP: Discocorp BWS 742 CD: Music and Arts CD 733

LENNOX BERKELEY (1903-1989)

4 poems of saint teresa of avila

London 4 April 1948	Orchestra Goldsborough	LP: BBC Records REGL 368 LP: Arabesque 8070

JOHANNES BRAHMS (1833-1897)

alto rhapsody

London 19 December 1947	LPO Chorus LPO Krauss	78: Decca K 1847-1848/ AK 1847-1848 45: Decca CEP 569 LP: Decca LXT 2850/ACL 306/AKF 1-7 LP: London LLP 903/5098/R 23183/STS 15201 CD: Decca 421 2992/433 4772/433 8022 CD: Gala GL 307
Copenhagen 6 October 1949	Danish Radio Orchestra & Chorus Busch	LP: Danacord DACO 114 CD: Danacord DACOCD 301
Oslo 14 October 1949	Oslo Philharmonic Orchestra & Chorus Tuxen	Unpublished radio broadcast

4 ernste gesänge

London 7-8 October 1947	Spurr	78: Decca K 1742-1743 Never published: matrices destroyed
London 12 January 1949	BBC SO Sargent	LP: Decca LXT 6934/414 0951 CD: Decca 433 4722/433 8022 Performed in Sargent's orchestration
New York 8 January 1950	Newmark	Unpublished radio broadcast

London
17 July
1950
	Newmark	78: Decca AX 563-564
		LP: Decca LW 5094/LXT 2556/
		    ACL 306/AKF 1-7
		LP: London LD 9097/LLP 271/
		    5020/R 23183
		CD: Decca 421 2992/433 4772/433 8022

2 lieder with viola obbligato: gestillte sehnsucht; geistliches wiegenlied

London 9 December 1947- 22 June 1948	Spurr Gilbert, viola	Decca unpublished <u>Matrices destroyed</u>
London 15 February 1949	Spurr Gilbert, viola	78: Decca K 2289 78: London T 5647 45: Decca CEP 720 LP: Decca LXT 2850/ACL 306/AKF 1-7 LP: London LLP 903/5098/R 23183 CD: Decca 421 2992/433 4772/433 8022

liebeslieder-walzer

Edinburgh 2 September 1952	Seefried, Patzak, Günter, Curzon, Gal	LP: Decca 417 6341 CD: Decca 425 9952

zum schluss/neue liebeslieder-walzer

Edinburgh 2 September 1952	Seefried, Patzak, Günter, Curzon, Gal	LP: Decca 417 6341 CD: Decca 425 9952

3 vocal quartets: an die heimat; der abend; fragen

Edinburgh 2 September 1952	Seefried, Patzak, Günter, Gal	Unpublished radio broadcast

auf dem see (blauer himmel, blauer wogen)

London 2 April 1952	Stone	LP: BBC Records REGL 368 LP: Arabesque 8070

botschaft (wehe lüftchen, lind und lieblich)

Edinburgh 7 September 1949	Walter	LP: Discocorp BWS 707 LP: Decca 6BB 197-198/414 6111 CD: Decca 411 6112/433 4762/433 8022
London 19 December 1949	Spurr	45: Decca 45-71130/CEP 719 LP: Decca LXT 2850/ACL 306/AKF 1-7 LP: London LLP 903/5098/R 23183 CD: Decca 430 0962/433 4712/433 8022

es schauen die blumen

London 2 April 1952	Stone	LP: BBC Records REGL 368 LP: Arabesque 8070

feinsliebchen, du sollst mir nicht barfuss geh'n/deutsche volkslieder

London 30 June 1944	Moore <u>Sung in English</u>	LP: EMI HLM 7145 CD: EMI CZS 569 7432 CD: Appian APR 5544 <u>HMV test recording</u>

immer leiser wird mein schlummer

Edinburgh 7 September 1949	Walter	LP: Discocorp BWS 707 LP: Decca 6BB 197-198/414 6111 CD: Decca 414 6112/433 4762/433 8022

der jäger (mein lieb ist ein jäger und grün ist sein kleid)

London 2 April 1952	Stone	LP: BBC Records REGL 368 LP: Arabesque 8070

liebestreu (o versenk, o versenk dein leid)

London 30 June 1944	Moore <u>Sung in English</u>	LP: EMI HLM 7145 CD: EMI CZS 569 7432 CD: Appian APR 5544 <u>HMV test recording</u>

ruhe süssliebchen/die schöne magelone

London	Stone	LP: BBC Records REGL 368
2 April		LP: Arabesque 8070
1952		

sapphische ode (rosen brach ich nachts)

London   Spurr   45: Decca 45-71130/CEP 719
19 December   LP: Decca LXT 2850/ACL 306/
1949   PA 172/AKF 1-7
                                       LP: London LLP 903/5098/R 23183
                                       CD: Decca 430 0962/433 4712/
                                            433 8022/458 8702

sonntag (so hab' ich doch die ganze woche)

Milan   Favaretto   LP: Rococo 5265
6 February   LP: Rodolphe RP 12407
1951   CD: Laserlight 14 262

der tod das ist die kühle nacht

Edinburgh   Walter   LP: Discocorp BWS 707
7 September   LP: Decca 6BB 197-198/414 6111
1949   CD: Decca 414 6112/433 4762/433 8022

von ewiger liebe (dunkel, wie dunkel, in wald und in flur)

Edinburgh 7 September 1949	Walter	LP: Discocorp BWS 707 LP: Decca 6BB 197-198/414 6111 CD: Decca 414 6112/433 4762/433 8022
Copenhagen 6 October 1949	Spurr	LP: Danacord DACO 114 CD: Danacord DACOCD 301 <u>Opening bars missing</u>

wir wandelten, wir zwei zusammen

Copenhagen 6 October 1949	Spurr	LP: Danacord DACO 114 CD: Danacord DACOCD 301 <u>Opening bars missing</u>
London 2 April 1952	Stone	Unpublished radio broadcast <u>Recording incomplete</u>

142 Ferrier

FRANK BRIDGE (1879-1941)

go not, happy day!

London
6 June
1952
	Stone	LP: Decca LW 5353/LX 3133/ACL 306/
		     AKF 1-7/PA 172
		LP: London LPS 1032/R 23187
		CD: Decca 430 0612/430 0962/433 4732/
		    433 8022/458 8702

BENJAMIN BRITTEN (1913-1976)

the rape of lucretia

Amsterdam 4-5 October 1946	Role of Lucretia Cross, Ritchie, Pollak, Pears, Donlevy, O.Kraus, Brannigan Glyndebourne Opera Orchestra Britten	LP: Discocorp IGI 369 CD: Music and Arts CD 901 Abridged recording but including all major scenes with Lucretia
London 11 October 1946	Cross, Ritchie, Pollak, Pears, Donlevy, O.Kraus, Brannigan Glyndebourne Opera Orchestra Goodall	Unpublished radio broadcast Excerpts LP: BBC Records REGL 368 LP: Arabesque 8070 CD: Memoir CDMOIR 440

spring symphony

Amsterdam 14 July 1949	Vincent, Pears Dutch Radio Choir Concertgebouw Orchestra Van Beinum	CD: Decca 440 0632 World premiere performance

abraham and isaac, canticle

London 4 February 1952	Pears Britten, piano	Unpublished radio broadcast Recording may have been erased

ERNEST CHAUSSON (1855-1899)

poème de l'amour et de la mer

Manchester 9 March 1951	Hallé Barbirolli	LP: Decca 414 0951 CD: Decca 433 4722/433 8022

EDWARD ELGAR (1857-1934)

the dream of gerontius, excerpts (my task is o'er/it is because then thou didst fear)

London 30 June 1944	Moore, piano	LP: EMI HLM 7145 CD: EMI CZS 769 7432 CD: Appian APR 5544 HMV test recording: excerpt incomplete

HOWARD FERGUSON (Born 1908)

discovery, song cycle

London 12 January 1953	Lush	LP: Decca 6BB 197-198 CD: Decca 430 0612/433 4722/433 8022

CHRISTOPH WILLIBALD GLUCK (1714-1787)

orfeo ed euridice

London 23 June 1947	Role of Orfeo Ayars, Vlachopoulos Glyndebourne Festival Chorus Southern Philharmonic Orchestra Stiedry	78: Decca K 1656-1662/AK 1656-1662 LP: Decca LXT 2893/ACL 293/417 1821 LP: London LLP 924/5103 CD: Decca 433 4682/433 8022 CD: Dutton CDEA 5015 Dutton edition restores material which was omitted from the LP issues of this abridged recording Excerpts LP: Decca LW 5225/PA 172 LP: London LD 9229
New York 17 March 1950	Ayars, Kinloch Little Orchestra Society & Chorus Scherman	Unpublished radio broadcast Recording stored in collection of New York Public Library
Amsterdam 10 July 1951	Koeman, Duval Netherlands Opera Orchestra & Chorus Bruck	LP: EMI RLS 725/2C151 25637-25638 CD: Verona 27016-27017 Excerpts LP: BBC Records REGL 368 LP: Arabesque 8070 CD: EMI CDH 761 0032

orfeo ed euridice, excerpt (che farò)

London 30 June 1944	Moore Sung in English	LP: EMI HLM 7145 CD: EMI CZS 769 7432 CD: Appian APR 5544 CD: Dutton CDLX 7024 HMV test recording

London
27 February
1946
	LSO
	Sargent
	Sung in English
		78: Decca K 1466
		78: London T 5434
		45: Decca 45-71034/CEP 724
		LP: Decca LW 5072/ACL 308/AKF 1-7/
		    PA 172/SPA 355
		LP: London LD 9066/LLP 1529/
		    5258/R 23185
		CD: Decca 430 0962/433 4702/
		    433 8022/458 2702
		CD: Memoir CDMOIR 440
		CD: Dutton CDLX 7020

Milan 6 February 1951	Favaretto	LP: Rococo 5265 LP: Rodolphe RP 12407 CD: Laserlight 14 262

ROYAL ALBERT HALL
(Manager: C. S. Taylor)

LONDON PHILHARMONIC ORCHESTRA

Conductor:
BRUNO WALTER

Thursday, November 13th 1947 at 7.30 p.m.

Programme One Shilling

PROGRAMME

Te Deum - - - - **Bruckner**

    Allegro
    Moderato
    Allegro
    Moderato
    Allegro
    Chorale—Fugue—Coda

Symphony No. 9 in D minor (Choral)   **Beethoven**

    Allegro, ma non troppo, un poco maestoso
    Molto vivace
    Adagio molto e cantabile
    Presto—Allegro ma non troppo—Allegro assai—Presto— Allegro assai—Allegro assai vivace (Alla marcia)— Andante maestoso—Adagio ma non troppo, ma divoto—Allegro energico, sempre ben marcato— Allegro ma non tanto—Prestissimo—Maestoso— Prestissimo

    ISOBEL BAILLIE, *Soprano*
    KATHLEEN FERRIER, *Contralto*
    HEDDLE NASH, *Tenor*
    WILLIAM PARSONS, *Baritone*

    THE LONDON PHILHARMONIC CHOIR
    (Chorus Master : FREDERIC JACKSON)

MAURICE GREENE (1696-1755)

o praise the lord!; i will lay me down in peace, arranged by roper

London	Moore	78: Columbia DB 2152
30 September		45: Columbia SED 5530
1944		LP: EMI HLM 7002
		LP: Angel 60203
		CD: EMI CDH 761 0032/CZS 769 7432
		CD: Appian APR 5544
		CD: Memoir CDMOIR 440

FRANZ XAVER GRUBER (1787-1863)

stille nacht, heilige nacht

London	Boyd Neel	78: Decca M 622
6 August	Orchestra	78: London T 5052
1948	Neel	45: Decca 45-71036
	Sung in English	45: London 45-40166
		LP: Decca LXT 6934/PA 172
		CD: Decca 433 4732/433 8022

GEORGE FRIDERIC HANDEL (1685-1759)

admeto, excerpt (cangio d'aspetto)

Oslo 16 October 1949	Spurr <u>Sung in English</u>	LP: Decca LXT 5324/ACL 310/AKF 1-7 LP: London LLP 1670/5291/R 23187 CD: Decca 433 4732/433 8022

atalanta, excerpt (come alla tortorella langue)

Oslo 16 October 1949	Spurr <u>Sung in English</u>	45: Decca CEP 587 LP: Decca LXT 5324/ACL 310/AKF 1-7 LP: London LLP 1670/5291/R 23187 CD: Decca 433 4732/433 8022
Milan 6 February 1951	Favaretto <u>Sung in English</u>	LP: Rococo 5265 LP: Rodolophe RP 12407 CD: Laserlight 14262

judas maccabaeus, excerpt (father of heaven)

London 8 October 1952	LPO Boult	45: Decca CEP 723 LP: Decca LW 5076/LXT 2757/ LXT 5382/414 6231 LP: London LD 9088/LLP 688/5083 CD: Decca 414 6232/433 4742/433 8022 CD: Gala GL 307 <u>Other LP reissues with stereo re-recording</u> <u>of orchestral accompaniment on Decca</u> <u>SXL 2234/SDD 433/SDD 286/AKF 1-7/</u> <u>SPA 531/SPA 566</u>

messiah, excerpt (ou thou that tellest glad tidings of zion)

London 8 October 1952	LPO Boult	45: Decca 45-71038/CEP 550 LP: Decca LW 5076/LXT 2757/ LXT 5382/414 6231 LP: London LD 9088/LLP 688/5083 CD: Decca 414 6232/433 4742/433 8022 CD: Gala GL 307 <u>Other reissues with stereo re-recording</u> <u>of orchestral accompaniment on Decca</u> <u>SEC 5099/SXL 2234/SDD 286/AKF 1-7/</u> <u>SPA 297/SPA 531/DPA 552-553</u>

messiah, excerpt (he was despised)

London 8 October 1952	LPO Boult	45: Decca CEP 550 LP: Decca LW 5075/LW 5225/LXT 2757/ LXT 5382/PA 172/SDD 286/414 6231 LP: London LD 9088/LD 9229/LLP 688/5083 CD: Decca 414 6232/433 4742/433 8022 CD: Gala GL 307 Other reissues with stereo re-recording of orchestral accompaniment on Decca SEC 5099/SXL 2234/AKF 1-7/SPA 448/SPA 531

ottone, excerpts (la speranza è giunta in porto; vieni o figlio, arranged by somervell)

London 20 April 1945	Moore Sung in English	78: Columbia DX 1194 45: Columbia SED 5526/SCD 2143 LP: EMI HLM 7002 LP: Angel 60203 CD: EMI CDH 761 0032 CD: Memoir CDMOIR 440 CD: Appian APR 5544

rodelinda, excerpt (dove sei amato bene)

London 27 February 1946	LSO Sargent Sung in English	78: Decca K 1466 78: London T 5434 45: Decca 45-71034 LP: Decca LW 5072/ACL 308/AKF 1-7/PA 172 LP: London LD 9066/LLP 1529/5258/R 23185 CD: Decca 430 0962/433 4702/ 433 8022/458 8702 CD: Memoir CDMOIR 440 CD: Dutton CDLX 7020

samson, excerpt (return o god of hosts!)

London 8 October 1952	LPO Boult	45: Decca 45-71038/CEP 723 LP: Decca LW 5076/LXT 2757/ LXT 5382/414 6231 LP: London LD 9088/LLP 688/5083 CD: Decca 414 6232/433 4742/433 8022 CD: Gala GL 307 Other LP reissues with stereo re-recording of orchestral accompaniment on Decca SXL 2234/SDD 286/AKF 1-7/SPA 531

semele, excerpt (where'er you walk)

Milan 6 February 1951	Favaretto	LP: Rococo 5265 LP: Rodolophe RP 12407 CD: Laserlight 14262

serse, excerpt (ombra mai fu)

London 14 May 1948	LSO Sargent	Decca unpublished Matrices destroyed

London
7 October
1948
	LSO
	Sargent
		78: Decca K 2135
		78: London T 5349
		45: Decca 45-71039
		45: London D 18060
		LP: Decca LW 5072/ACL 308/AKF 1-7
		LP: London LD 9066/LPS 104/LLP 1529/
		    5258/R 23185
		CD: Decca 430 0962/433 4702/
		    433 8022/458 8702

MAURICE JACOBSON

song of songs

London 3 November 1947	Stone	Unpublished radio broadcast National Sound Archive

ADOLF JENSEN (1837-1879)

altar

Oslo 16 October 1949	Spurr	45: Decca CEP 587 LP: Decca LXT 5324/AKF 1-7/PA 172 LP: London LLP 1670/5291 CD: Decca 433 4732/433 8022 With spoken introduction by Ferrier

ANTONIO LOTTI (1667-1740)

arminio, excerpt (pur dicesti)

Milan 6 February 1951	Favaretto	LP: Rococo 5265 LP: Rodolophe RP 12407 CD: Laserlight 14262

GUSTAV MAHLER (1860-1911)

symphony no 2 "resurrection"

Amsterdam 12 July 1951	Vincent Toonkunstkoor Concertgebouw Orchestra Klemperer	LP: Discocorp IGI 374 LP: Decca D264 D2 CD: Decca 425 9702 CD: Verona 27062 <u>Excerpt</u> CD: Verona 27076

symphony no 3

London 29 November 1947	Choirs BBCSO Boult	Unpublished radio broadcast <u>Music Performance Centre</u>

kindertotenlieder

London 4 October 1949	VPO Walter	78: Columbia LX 8939-8941 LP: Columbia 33C 1009 LP: Columbia (USA) ML 2187/ML 4980/ 3226 0016 LP: Angel 60203 LP: EMI HLM 7002 CD: EMI CDH 761 0032 CD: Gala GL 307
Amsterdam 12 July 1951	Concertgebouw Orchestra Klemperer	LP: Decca 417 6341 CD: Decca 425 9952

154 Ferrier

das lied von der erde

New York 18 January 1948	Svanholm NYPSO Walter	Unpublished radio broadcast <u>Von der Schönheit & Der Abschied</u> LP: Discocorp IGI 374
Manchester 22 April 1952	Lewis Hallé Barbirolli	Unpublished radio broadcast

Vienna
15-16
May
1952
	Patzak
	VPO
	Walter
		LP: Decca LXT 2721-2722/LXT 5576/
		    LXT 6278/ACL 305/AKF 1-7/414 1941
		LP: London LLP 625-626/5069-5070/
		    A 4212/R 23182/STS 15200
		CD: Decca 414 1942

ich atmet' einen linden duft/rückert-lieder

Vienna
20 May
1952
	VPO
	Walter
		LP: Decca LW 5123/LXT 2721/
		    ACL 318/AKF 1-7
		LP: London LP 9137/LLP 625/5069/
		    A 4212/STS 15202
		CD: Decca 421 2992/433 4772/433 8022/
		    448 1502/455 2952

ich bin der welt abhanden gekommen/rückert-lieder

Vienna
20 May
1952
	VPO
	Walter
		LP: Decca LW 5123/LXT 2721/
		    ACL 318/AKF 1-7
		LP: London LP 9137/LLP 625/5069/
		    A 4212/STS 15202
		CD: Decca 421 2992/433 4772/433 8022/
		    448 1502/455 2952

um mitternacht/rückert-lieder

Vienna
20 May
1952
	VPO
	Walter
		LP: Decca LW 5123/LW 5225/LXT 2721/
		    ACL 318/AKF 1-7/PA 172
		LP: London LD 9137/LD 9229/LLP 625/
		    A 4212/5069/STS 15202
		CD: Decca 421 2992/430 0962/433 4772/
		    433 8022/448 1502/455 2952/458 8702

FELIX MENDELSSOHN-BARTHOLDY (1809-1847)

elijah, excerpt (o rest in the lord)

London
2 September
1946
	Boyd Neel
	Orchestra
	Neel
		78: Decca K 1556
		78: London D 18060
		45: Decca 45-71039/CEP 724
		LP: Decca LW 5072/ACL 308/AKF 1-7/
		     SPA 316/SPA 433
		LP: London LD 9066/LLP 1529/
		     5258/R 23185
		CD: Decca 430 0962/433 4702/433 8022
		CD: Memoir CDMOIR 440
		CD: Dutton CDLX 7025

elijah, excerpt (woe unto them!)

London 2 September 1946	Boyd Neel Orchestra Neel	78: Decca K 1556 45: Decca 45-71112/CEP 724 LP: Decca ACL 308/AKF 1-7 LP: London R 23185 CD: Decca 430 0962/433 4702/ 433 8022/458 8702 CD: Memoir CDMOIR 440 CD: Dutton CDLX 7025

gruss/leise zieht durch mein gemüt

London 21 September 1945	Baillie Moore Sung in English	78: Columbia DB 2194 45: Columbia SED 5526 LP: EMI HLM 7002/HQM 1072 LP: Angel 60044/60203 CD: Appian APR 5544 CD: Memoir CDMOIR 440

ich wollt' meine lieb'

London 21 September 1945	Baillie Moore Sung in English	78: Columbia DB 2194 45: Columbia SED 5526 LP: EMI HLM 7002 LP: Angel 60203 CD: EMI CDH 761 0032 CD: Appian APR 5544 CD: Memoir CDMOIR 440

156 Ferrier

CLAUDIO MONTEVERDI (1567-1643)

l'arianna, excerpt (lasciatemi morir)

Milan	Favaretto	LP: Rococo 5265
6 February		LP: Rodolphe RP 12407
1951		CD: Laserlight 14262

KATIE MOSS (Born 1881)

the floral dance

New York	Ferrier, piano	LP: BBC Records REGL 368
May		LP: Arabesque 8070
1949		<u>Privately recorded at an informal party: excerpts from other songs from the same source apparently also survive</u>

HUBERT PARRY (1848-1918)

love is a bable/english lyrics

| Edinburgh
26 August
1948 | Moore | LP: BBC Records REGL 368
LP: Arabesque 8070 |

| Milan
6 February
1951 | Favaretto | LP: Rococo 5265
LP: Rodolphe RP 12407
CD: Laserlight 14262 |

| London
6 June
1952 | Stone | LP: Decca LX 3133/LW 5353/
    ACL 310/AKF 1-7
LP: London LPS 1032/R 23187
CD: Decca 430 0612/433 4732/433 8022 |

GIOVANNI PERGOLESI (1710-1736)

stabat mater, arranged by scott

| London
28 May
1946 | Taylor
Boyd Neel
Orchestra
Henderson | 78: Decca K 1517-1521/AK 1517-1521
LP: Decca LXT 6907/417 4661
CD: Decca 433 4702/433 8022
<u>Sancta mater & Fac ut portem</u>
CD: Memoir CDMOIR 440
<u>Choral sections recorded on 8 May 1946</u> |

158 Ferrier

HENRY PURCELL (1659-1695)

come ye sons of art, excerpt (sound the trumpet)

London 21 September 1945	Baillie Moore	78: Columbia DB 2201 45: Columbis SED 5530 LP: EMI HLM 7002 LP: Angel 60203 CD: EMI CDH 761 0032 CD: Appian APR 5544 CD: Memoir CDMOIR 440

the fairy queen, excerpt (hark the echoing air)

Oslo 16 October 1949	Spurr	LP: Decca LXT 5324/ACL 310/AKF 1-7 LP: London LLP 1670/5291/R 23187 CD: Decca 433 4732/433 8022
Milan 6 February 1951	Favaretto	LP: Rococo 5265 LP: Rodolphe RP 12407 CD: Laserlight 14262

the indian queen, excerpt (let us wander)

London 21 September 1945	Baillie Moore	78: Columbia DB 2201 45: Columbia SED 5530 LP: EMI HLM 7002 LP: Angel 60203 CD: EMI CDH 761 0032 CD: Appian APR 5544 CD: Memoir CDMOIR 440

king arthur, excerpt (shepherd leave decoying!)

London 21 September 1945	Baillie Moore	78: Columbia DB 2201 45: Columbia SED 5530 LP: EMI HLM 7002 LP: Angel 60203 CD: EMI CDH 761 0032 CD: Appian APR 5544 CD: Memoir CDMOIR 440

ROGER QUILTER (1877-1953)

the fair house of joy

London 11 December 1951	Spurr	45: Decca 45-71139 LP: Decca LX 3098/ACL 309/AKF 1-7 LP: London LPS 538/5411/R 23186 CD: Decca 417 1922/433 4752/ 433 8022/458 8702

now sleeps the crimson petal

London
10 December
1951
	Spurr	78: Decca M 680
		45: Decca 45-71139/CEP 726
		LP: Decca LX 3098/BR 3052/
		    ACL 309/AKF 1-7
		LP: London LPS 538/5411/R 23186
		CD: Decca 417 1922/433 4752/
		    433 8022/458 8702

to daisies

London 11 December 1951	Spurr	78: Decca M 680 45: Decca 45-71139 LP: Decca ACL 309/AKF 1-7 LP: London R 23186 CD: Decca 417 1922/433 4752/ 433 8022/458 8702

EDMUND RUBBRA (1901-1986)

3 psalms: o lord rebuke me not!; the lord is my shepherd; praise ye the lord!

London 3 November 1947	Stone	Unpublished radio broadcast <u>National Sound Archive</u>
London 12 January 1953	Lush	LP: Decca 6BB 197-198 CD: Decca 430 0612/433 4722/433 8022

FRANZ SCHUBERT (1797-1828)

an die musik (du holde kunst, in wieviel grauen stunden)

London	Spurr	78: Decca M 652
14 February		45: Decca CEP 663/CEP 719
1949		LP: Decca LW 5098/ACL 307/AKF 1-7/
		PA 172/SPA 524
		LP: London LD 9099/LLP 1529/
		5258/R 23184
		CD: Decca 430 0962/433 4712/
		433 8022/458 8702

du bist die ruh'

Edinburgh	Walter	LP: Discocorp BWS 707
7 September		LP: Decca 6BB 197-198/414 6111
1949		CD: Decca 414 6112/433 4762/433 8022

du liebst mich nicht (mein herz ist zerrissen)

Edinburgh	Walter	LP: Discocorp BWS 707
7 September		LP: Decca 6BB 197-198/414 6111
1949		CD: Decca 414 6112/433 4762/433 8022
London	Britten	CD: Decca 433 4712/433 8022
4 February		<u>Recording incomplete</u>
1952		

ganymed (wie im morgenglanze du rings mich anglühst)

London	Britten	CD: Decca 433 4712/433 8022
4 February		
1952		

gretchen am spinnrade (meine ruh' ist hin, mein herz ist schwer)

London 14 March 1947	Spurr	78: Decca K 1632 78: London T 5435 45: Decca CEP 663 LP: Decca LW 5098/ACL 307/AKF 1-7 LP: London LD 9099/LLP 1529/ 5258/R 23184 CD: Decca 430 0962/433 4712/433 8022

die junge nonne (wie braust durch die wipfel der heulende sturm)

London 14 March 1947	Spurr	78: Decca K 1632 78: London T 5435 45: Decca CEP 663 LP: Decca LW 5098/ACL 307/AKF 1-7 LP: London LD 9099/LLP 1529/ 5258/R 23184 CD: Decca 430 0962/433 4712/433 8022 CD: Preiser 89231
Edinburgh 7 September 1949	Walter	LP: Discocorp BWS 707 LP: Decca 6BB 197-198/414 6111 CD: Decca 414 6112/433 4762/433 8022
London 29 September 1952	Stone	Unpublished radio broadcast

lachen und weinen

Milan 6 February 1951	Favaretto	LP: Rococo 5265 LP: Rodolphe RP 12407 CD: Laserlight 14262
London 4 February 1952	Britten	CD: Decca 433 4712/433 8022

162 Ferrier

der musensohn (durch feld und wald zu schweifen)

London 14 February 1949	Spurr	Decca unpublished <u>Matrices destroyed</u>

London
19 December
1949
	Spurr	78: Decca M 652
		45: Decca CEP 663/CEP 719
		LP: Decca LW 5098/ACL 307/AKF 1-7/
		    PA 172/SPA 524
		LP: London LD 9099/LLP 1529/
		    5258/R 23184
		CD: Decca 430 0962/433 4712/433 8022

rastlose liebe (dem schnee dem regen dem winde entgegen)

London 29 September 1952	Stone	LP: BBC Records REGL 368 LP: Arabesque 8070

romanze (der vollmond strahlt)

Edinburgh 7 September 1949	Walter	LP: Discocorp BWS 707 LP: Decca 6BB 197-198/414 6111 CD: Decca 414 6112/433 4762/ 433 8022/458 8702
London 29 September 1952	Stone	Unpublished radio broadcast

suleika I (was bedeutet die bewegung?)

Edinburgh 7 September 1949	Walter	LP: Discocorp BWS 707 LP: Decca 6BB 197-198/414 6111 CD: Decca 414 6112/433 4762/433 8022
London 29 September 1952	Stone	Unpublished radio broadcast

der tod und das mädchen (vorüber, ach vorüber!)

Edinburgh 7 September 1949	Walter	LP: Discocorp BWS 707 LP: Decca 6BB 197-198/414 6111 CD: Decca 414 6112/433 4762/433 8022

wasserflut/die winterreise (manche trän' aus meinen augen)

London 29 September 1952	Stone	LP: BBC Records REGL 368 LP: Arabesque 8070

ROBERT SCHUMANN (1810-1856)

frauenliebe und -leben, song cycle

Edinburgh 7 September 1949	Walter	LP: Discocorp DIS 3700/BWS 707 LP: Decca 6BB 197-198/414 6111 CD: Decca 414 6112/433 4762/433 8022

London
12-14
July
1950
	Newmark	LP: Decca LW 5089/LXT 2556/ACL 307/
		    AKF 1-7/DPA 624-625
		LP: London LD 9098/LLP 271/
		    5020/R 23184
		CD: Decca 433 4712/433 8022
		Er der Herrlichste von allen
		CD: Decca 458 8702

2 lieder: widmung; volksliedchen

London 14 July 1950	Newmark	45: Decca 45-71130/CEP 719 LP: Decca LW 5098/ACL 307/AKF 1-7 LP: London LD 9099/LLP 1529/ 5258/R 23184 CD: Decca 433 4712/433 8022

YURI SHAPORIN (1889-1966)

on the field of kulikovo, symphonic cantata

London 7 November 1945	Finneberg, Titterton, R.Jones BBC SO and Chorus Coates Sung in English	Unpublished radio broadcast National Sound Archive

CHARLES VILLIERS STANFORD (1852-1924)

the fairy lough

Milan 6 February 1951	Favaretto	LP: Rococo 5265 LP: Rodolphe RP 12407 CD: Laserlight 14262
London 5 June 1952	Stone	LP: Decca LX 3133/LW 5353/ ACL 310/AKF 1-7 LP: London LPS 1032/R 23187 CD: Decca 430 0612/433 4732/433 8022

a soft day

London 5 June 1952	Stone	LP: Decca LX 3133/LW 5353/ ACL 310/AKF 1-7 LP: London LPS 1032/R 23187 CD: Decca 430 0612/433 4732/433 8022

RALPH VAUGHAN WILLIAMS (1872-1958)

silent noon

London 6 June 1952	Stone	LP: Decca LX 3133/LW 5353/ ACL 310/AKF 1-7 LP: London LPS 1032/R 23187 CD: Decca 430 0612/433 4732/433 8022

PETER WARLOCK (1894-1930)

songs: sleep; pretty ring time

London	Stone	LP: Decca LX 3133/LW 5353/
6 June		ACL 310/AKF 1-7
1952		LP: London LPS 1032/R 23187
		CD: Decca 430 0612/433 4732/433 8022

HUGO WOLF (1860-1903)

4 mörike-lieder: verborgenheit; auf ein altes bild; der gärtner; auf einer wanderung

Oslo	Spurr	LP: Decca LXT 5324/ACL 307/AKF 1-7
16 October		LP: London LLP 1670/5291/R 23187
1949		CD: Decca 433 4732/433 8022

WILLIAM WORDSWORTH (1908-1988)

3 songs: red skies; clouds; the wind

London	Lush	LP: Decca 6BB 197-198
12 January		CD: Decca 430 0612/433 433 4722/433 8022
1953		

MISCELLANEOUS AND TRADITIONAL
Various arrangers

blow the wind southerly

London	Spurr	78: Decca F 9300
10 February		78: London R 10102
1949		45: Decca 45-71135/CEP 725
		LP: Decca LX 3040/LW 5225/BR 3052/
		ACL 309/AKF 1-7/PA 172/SPA 205/
		ECS 2178/DPA 627-628
		LP: London LD 9229/LPS 48/5411/R 23186
		CD: Decca 417 1922/430 0962/433 4752/
		433 8022/458 8702

ca' the yowes

London	Newmark	78: Decca M 657
17 July		45: Decca 45-71072/CEP 5508
1950		LP: Decca ACL 309/AKF 1-7
		LP: London R 23186
		LP: EMI EX 769 7411
		CD: Decca 417 1922/433 4752/433 8022

Milan	Favaretto	LP: Rococo 5265
6 February		LP: Rodolphe RP 12407
1951		CD: Laserlight 14262

come you not from newcastle?

London	Stone	LP: Decca LX 3133/LW 5353/ACL 310/
6 June		AKF 1-7/PA 172
1952		LP: London LPS 1032/R 23187
		CD: Decca 430 0612/430 0962/
		433 4732/433 8022

down by the salley gardens

London	Spurr	78: London R 10104
11 February		45: Decca 45-71135/CEP 518/CEP 725
1949		LP: Decca LX 3040/BR 3052/
		ACL 309/AKF 1-7
		LP: London LPS 48/5411/R 23186
		CD: Decca 417 1922/433 4752/
		433 8022/458 8702

168 Ferrier

drink to me only

London	Spurr	78: Decca M 679
12 December		45: Decca 45-71035/CEP 718/CEP 726
1951		LP: Decca LX 3098/BR 3052/
		ACL 309/AKF 1-7
		LP: London LPS 538/5411/R 23186
		CD: Decca 417 1922/433 4752/
		433 8022/458 8702

the fidgety bairn

London	Newmark	78: Decca M 657
17 July		45: Decca CEP 5508
1950		LP: Decca ACL 309/AKF 1-7
		LP: London R 23186
		CD: Decca 417 1922/433 4752/433 8022

have you seen but a whyte lillie grow?

London	Spurr	78: London R 10103
10 February		45: Decca CEP 725
1949		LP: Decca LX 3040/BR 3052/
		ACL 309/AKF 1-7
		LP: London LPS 48/5411/R 23186
		CD: Decca 417 1922/433 4752/433 8022

i have a bonnet trimmed with blue

London	Spurr	45: Decca 45-71108
10 December		LP: Decca LX 3098/BR 3052/
1951		ACL 309/AKF 1-7
		LP: London LPS 538/5411/R 23186
		CD: Decca 417 1922/433 4752/433 8022

i know where i'm going

London	Spurr	78: Decca M 681
11 December		45: Decca CEP 726
1951		LP: Decca LX 3098/BR 3052/
		ACL 309/AKF 1-7
		LP: London LPS 538/5411/R 23186
		CD: Decca 417 1922/433 4752/
		433 8022/458 8702

i will walk with my love

London   Spurr   78: Decca M 681
10 December   45: Decca 45-71108/CEP 725
1951   LP: Decca LX 3098/BR 3052/
                                    ACL 309/AKF 1-7
                                LP: London LPS 538/5411/R 23186
                                CD: Decca 417 1922/433 4752/433 8022

the keel row

London   Spurr   78: Decca F 9300
10 February   78: London R 10102
1949   45: Decca 45-71132
                                LP: Decca LX 3040/ACL 309/AKF 1-7/
                                    PA 172/DPA 627-628
                                LP: London LPS 48/5411/R 23186
                                CD: Decca 417 1922/430 0962/
                                    433 4752/433 8022

kitty my love

London   Stone   LP: Decca LX 3133/LW 5353/ACL 310/
6 June   AKF 1-7/PA 172
1952   LP: London LPS 1032/R 23187
                                CD: Decca 430 0612/430 0962/
                                    433 4732/433 8022

the lover's curse

London   Spurr   78: London R 10104
11 February   LP: Decca LX 3040/BR 3052/
1949   ACL 309/AKF 1-7
                                LP: London LPS 48/5411/R 23186
                                CD: Decca 417 1992/433 4752/433 8022

ma bonny lad

London   Spurr   78: Decca F 9300
10 February   78: London R 10102
1949   45: Decca 45-71135/CEP 725
                                LP: Decca LX 3040/BR 3052/ACL 309/
                                    AKF 1-7/PA 172
                                LP: London LPS 48/5411/R 23186
                                CD: Decca 417 1922/430 0962/433 4752/
                                    433 8022/458 8702

170 Ferrier

mad bess of bedlam

Oslo	Spurr	45: Decca CEP 5508
16 October		LP: Decca ACL 310/AKF 1-7
1949		CD: Decca 433 4732/433 8022

my boy willie

London	Spurr	45: Decca 45-71108
10 December		LP: Decca LX 3098/ACL 309/AKF 1-7
1951		LP: London LPS 538/5411/R 23186
		CD: Decca 417 1922/433 4752/433 8022

o come all ye faithful

London	Boyd Neel	78: Decca M 622
6 August	Orchestra	78: London T 5052
1948	Neel	45: Decca 45-71036
		45: London 45-40166
		LP: Decca LXT 6934/PA 172
		CD: Decca 433 4732/433 8022

o waly waly

London	Spurr	45: Decca 45-71072/CEP 726
10 December		LP: Decca LX 3098/BR 3052/
1951		ACL 309/AKF 1-7
		LP: London LPS 538/5411/R 23186
		CD: Decca 417 1922/433 4752/433 8022
London	Stone	LP: Decca LX 3133/LW 5353
6 June		LP: London LPS 1032
1952		CD: Decca 430 0612/433 4732/433 8022

over the mountains

London	Spurr	45: Decca 45-71139
12 December		LP: Decca LX 3098/ACL 309/AKF 1-7
1951		LP: London LPS 538/5411/R 23186
		CD: Decca 417 1922/433 4752/433 8022

the spanish lady

Milan 6 February 1951	Favaretto	LP: Rococo 5265 LP: Rodolphe RP 12407 LP: BBC Records REGL 368 LP: Arabesque 8070 CD: Laserlight 14262

the stuttering lovers

London 10 December 1951	Spurr	78: Decca M 681 45: Decca 45-71108 LP: Decca LX 3098/ACL 309/AKF 1-7 LP: London LPS 538/5411/R 23186 CD: Decca 417 1922/433 4752/433 8022

turn ye to me

London 21 September 1945	Baillie Moore	Columbia unpublished <u>Matrix destroyed</u>

willow willow

London 11 February 1949	Spurr	78: London R 10103 45: Decca CEP 725 LP: Decca LX 3040/BR 3052/ ACL 309/AKF 1-7 LP: London LPS 48/5411/R 23186 CD: Decca 417 1922/433 4752/433 8022

ye banks and braes

London
12 December
1951
	Spurr	78: Decca M 679
		45: Decca 45-71035/CEP 718/CEP 726
		LP: Decca LX 3098/BR 3052/
		    ACL 309/AKF 1-7
		LP: London LPS 538/5411/R 23186
		CD: Decca 417 1922/433 4752/
		    433 8022/458 8702

INTERVIEWS

what the edinburgh festival has meant to me

Edinburgh
11 September
1949

LP: Decca 6BB 197-198/414 6111
CD: Decca 414 6112/433 4762/433 8022
Excerpt
LP: BBC Records REGL 368
LP: Arabesque 8070

interview with eric maclean

Montreal
10 March
1950

Unpublished radio broadcast
Excerpt
LP: BBC Records REGL 368
LP: Arabesque 8070

Giulietta Simionato
born 1910

LUDWIG VAN BEETHOVEN (1770-1827)

symphony no 9 "choral"

Milan 28 May 1949	Cecil, Prandelli, Siepi La Scala Orchestra & Chorus Furtwängler	Unpublished radio broadcast <u>Tape may not survive</u>

VINCENZO BELLINI (1801-1835)

i capuleti ed i montecchi

New York 14 October 1958	Role of Romeo Hurley, Cassilly, Flagello American Opera Society Orchestra and Chorus Gamson	LP: MRF Records MRF 19 CD: Melodram CDM 27509
New York 28 April 1964	Costa, Montal, Michalski American Opera Society Orchestra and Chorus Gardelli	Unpublished radio broadcast

i capuleti ed i montecchi, excerpt (deh tu bel anima!)

Rome July- August 1954	Santa Cecilia Orchestra Ghione	45: Decca 45-71094 LP: Decca LW 5139/LXT 5458/GRV 16 CD: Decca 440 4062 CD: Grandi voci GVS 08
Milan 20 December 1954	RAI Milano Orchestra Argento	LP: Voci celebri MPV 5 LP: Cetra LMR 5006 CD: Cetra CDMR 5006

norma

Mexico
23 May
1950
	Role of Adalgisa
	Callas, Baum,
	Moscona
	Bellas Artes
	Orchestra & Chorus
	Picco
		LP: Historical Recording Enterprises
		    HRE 252
		CD: Melodram MEL 26018/GM 20015
		Excerpts
		LP: Opus 91
		LP: Historical Recording Enterprises
		    HRE 219
		CD: Rodolphe RPC 32484-32487

Milan 7 December 1955	Callas, Del Monaco, Zaccaria La Scala Orchestra & Chorus Votto	LP: Limited Edition Society 103 LP: BJR Records BJR 147 LP: Cetra LO 31 LP: Impresario IE 3005 CD: Arkadia CD 517/CDHP 517 CD: Melodram MEL 26036 CD: Legendary LRCD 1007 CD: Gala GL 100.511 Excerpts LP: Melodram MEL 081
Milan 9 January 1965	Gencer, Prevedi, Zaccaria La Scala Orchestra & Chorus Gavazzeni	LP: Historical Recording Enterprises HRE 320 LP: Melodram MEL 468 LP: Great Opera Performances GFC 033 CD: Curcio OP 117
Paris 17 May 1965	Callas, Cecchele, Vinco Paris Opéra Orchestra & Chorus Prêtre	LP: Historical Recording Enterprises HRE 373 CD: Eklipse EKRCD 18 CD: Gala GL 100.523 The recording is a composite version from performances on 17 May and other dates: Simionato performed the role of Adalgisa on 17 May, on other dates it was taken by Fiorenza Cossotto

norma, excerpt (casta diva)

Rome September 1958	Santa Cecilia Orchestra & Chorus Paoletti	LP: Decca LXT 5643-5644/SXL 2281-2282 CD: Decca 440 4062 Test recording for a projected version of the opera in which Simionato was to have sung the title role

IRVING BERLIN (1888-1989)

annie get your gun, excerpt (anything you can do)

1960	Bastianini Instrumentalists	LP: Decca MET 201-203/SET 201-203/D247 D3 CD: Decca 421 0462 CD: Great Opera Performances GOP 742 <u>Insert for gala sequence in Decca's Karajan Fledermaus recording</u>

HECTOR BERLIOZ (1803-1869)

la damnation de faust

Naples 26 December 1964	Bondino, Bastianini, San Carlo Orchestra & Chorus Maag <u>Sung in Italian</u>	LP: Estro armonico EA 037 CD: Great Opera Performances GOP 776 Excerpts LP: Timaclub 77-78

les troyens

Milan 27 May 1960	<u>Role of Dido</u> Rankin, Cossotto, Del Monaco, Zaccaria La Scala Orchestra & Chorus Kubelik <u>Sung in Italian</u>	LP: Historical Recording Enterprises HRE 291 LP: Paragon DSV 52011 Excerpts CD: VAI Audio VAIA 1026

GEORGES BIZET (1838-1875)

Milan 26 December 1950	Role of Carmen Pagliughi, Berdini, Boriello RAI Milano Orchestra & Chorus Previtali Sung in Italian	Unpublished radio broadcast Recording incomplete
21 August 1953	Rizieri, Corelli, Protti Sung in Italian	Unpublished radio broadcast
Naples 19-30 December 1953	Jurinac, Corelli, Savarese San Carlo Orchestra & Chorus Rodzinski Sung in Italian	LP: Edizioni lirica EL 001
Vienna 8 October 1954	Güden, Gedda, Roux Wiener Singverein VSO Karajan	LP: Great Opera Performances GFC 026 CD: Melodram MEL 27012 CD: Gala GL 100.603
Milan 18 January 1955	Carteri, Di Stefano, Roux La Scala Orchestra & Chorus Karajan	LP: Morgan MOR 5502 LP: Cetra LO 22 LP: Discocorp RR 470 CD: Di Stefano GDS 102 Excerpts LP: Melodram MEL 078 CD: Grandi voci GVS 08
Rio 17 August 1956	Salgado, Del Monaco, Guelfi Orchestra and Chorus Ghione Sung in Italian	Unpublished radio broadcast

carmen/continued

Rome 25 February 1957	Beltrami, Di Stefano, Mascherini Rome Opera Orchestra & Chorus Questa <u>Sung in Italian</u>	LP: Ed Smith UORC 303
Palermo 8 February 1959	Freni, Corelli, Guelfi Teatro Massimo Orchestra & Chorus Dervaux <u>Sung in Italian</u>	LP: Stradivarius STR 1003-1005 LP: Great Opera Performances GFC 030 CD: Great Opera Performances GOP 727 <u>Excerpts</u> CD: Melodram MEL 26020
Tokyo 19 February 1959	Tucci, Del Monaco, Colombo NHK Orchestra and Chorus Verchi <u>Sung in Italian</u>	LP: Legendary LR 190 LP: Melodram MEL 416
Verona July 1961	Scotto, Corelli, Bastianini Arena di Verona Orchestra & Chorus Molinari-Pradelli <u>Sung in Italian</u>	CD: Bongiovanni GAO 118-119
Rio 2 August 1961	Scotto, Corelli, Bastianini Orchestra & Chorus Molinari-Pradelli <u>Sung in Italian</u>	Unpublished radio broadcast

carmen, excerpt (l'amour est un oiseau rebelle)

Milan 4 May 1951	Milan SO Quadri <u>Sung in Italian</u>	78: Columbia (Italy) GQX 11503 LP: EMI 3C053 18031 LP: Timaclub 77-78
Rome July 1956	Santa Cecilia Orchestra Previtali	LP: Decca LXT 5458 CD: Decca 440 4062

ARRIGO BOITO (1842-1918)

nerone, act 3 and act 4 scene 2

Milan 10 June 1948	Role of Rubria Nelli, Ticozzi, Guarrera, Siepi La Scala Orchestra & Chorus Toscanini	LP: Morgan MOR 4801 LP: Hope Records HOPE 222 LP: Historical Recording Enterprises HRE 257 CD: Legato SRO 802

JOHANNES BRAHMS (1833-1897)

wiegenlied

1983	Sung in Italian	LP: Timaclub 77-78

FABIO CAMPANA (1819-1882)

m'hai tradito

18 December 1956	Bettarini	LP: Timaclub 77-78

LUIGI CHERUBINI (1760-1842)

medea

Milan 11 December 1961	Role of Neris Callas, Tosini, Vickers, Ghiaurov La Scala Orchestra & Chorus Schippers	LP: MRF Records MRF 102 LP: Cetra DOC 21 CD: Arkadia CDLSMH 34028/CDMP 428 Arkadia incorrectly dated 14 December
Milan 14 December 1961	Callas, Tosini, Vickers, Ghiaurov La Scala Orchestra & Chorus Schippers	CD: Ombra 520 Extracts only

FRANCESCO CILEA (1866-1950)

adriana lecouvreur

Naples 28 November 1959	Role of Principessa Olivero, Corelli, Bastianini San Carlo Orchestra & Chorus Rossi	LP: Morgan MOR 5901 LP: Ed Smith EJS 497 LP: MRF Records MRF 47 LP: Hope Records HOPE 246 LP: Melodram MEL 043 LP: Cetra DOC 19 LP: Discocorp IGI 294 LP: Replica RPL 2454-2456 CD: Melodram MEL 27009 CD: Phoenix PX 5022
Rome July 1961	Tebaldi, Del Monaco Fioravanti Santa Cecilia Orchestra & Chorus Capuana	LP: Decca MET 221-223/SET 221-223 LP: London OSA 13126 CD: Decca 430 2562

adriana lecouvreur, excerpt (acerba voluttà)

Reggio Calabria 1 July 1961	Orchestra Ziino	LP: Timaclub 77-78

l'arlesiana, excerpt (esser madre è un inferno)

Reggio Calabria 1 July 1961	Orchestra Ziino	LP: Timaclub 77-78

tu pur sei figlio

Reggio Calabria 1 July 1961	Orchestra Ziino	LP: Timaclub 77-78

DOMENICO CIMAROSA (1849-1901)

il matrimonio segreto

Florence 1950	Role of Fidalma Noni, Valletti, Bruscantini Maggio musicale Orchestra & Chorus Wolf-Ferrari	LP: Cetra LPC 1214/LPS 3214 CD: Cetra CDO 32 Excerpts LP: Cetra LPC 55064/LEC 36 CD: Grandi voci GVS 08

gli orazi e i curiazi

Milan 13 April 1952	Role of Curazio Vercelli, Spataro, Del Signore RAI Milano Orchestra & Chorus Giulini	CD: Melodram CDM 29500

SALZBURGER FESTSPIELE 1962

DER TROUBADOUR

OPER IN VIER AKTEN
TEXT VON SALVATORE CAMMARANO

MUSIK VON
GIUSEPPE VERDI

INSZENIERUNG UND MUSIKALISCHE LEITUNG
HERBERT VON KARAJAN

BÜHNENBILD
TEO OTTO

KOSTÜME
GEORGES WAKHEVITCH

ORCHESTER
DIE WIENER PHILHARMONIKER
CHOR DER WIENER STAATSOPER
EIN KAMMERCHOR DER SALZBURGER FESTSPIELE

DER TROUBADOUR

(in italienischer Sprache)

Oper in vier Akten (acht Bildern)
nach einem Drama des Antonio Garcia Gutierrez von Salvatore Cammarano

MUSIK VON GIUSEPPE VERDI

Der Graf von Luna	Ettore Bastianini
Leonore	Leontyne Price
Azucena, Zigeunerin	Giulietta Simionato
Manrico	Franco Corelli
Ferrando	Nicola Zaccaria
Ines	Laurence Dutoit
Ruiz	Siegfried Rudolf Frese
Ein alter Zigeuner	Rudolf Zimmer
Ein Bote	Kurt Equiluz

Gefährtinnen Leonores, Nonnen, Krieger, Diener des Grafen,
Zigeuner und Zigeunerinnen

Ort der Handlung: Arragon und Biskaya zu Beginn des XV. Jahrhunderts

Einstudierung der Chöre: Roberto Benaglio

Technische Einrichtung und Beleuchtung: Sepp Nordegg

Pause nach dem vierten Bild

Der offizielle Almanach „Salzburg — Festspiele 1962" ist auch für Sie der unentbehrliche Ratgeber
The official almanac "Salzburg Festivals 1962" is an indispensable guide for all Festival visitors
L'almanach officiel «Salzbourg Festival 1962» est indispensable à tous ceux qui s'intéressent au Festival

GAETONO DONIZETTI (1797-1848)

anna bolena

Milan 17 April 1957	Role of Giovanna Callas, Raimondi, Rossi-Lemeni La Scala Orchestra & Chorus Gavazzeni	LP: Morgan MOR 5703 LP: Ed Smith EJS 166 LP: BJR Records BJR 109 LP: MRF Records MRF 42 LP: Hope Records HOPE 226 LP: Cetra LO 53/DOC 22 LP: Replica ARPL 32493 LP: FWR 646 LP: Foyer FO 1014 CD: Replica RPCL 32029 CD: Arkadia CD 518/CDHP 518 CD: Melodram MEL 26010 CD: Great Opera Performances GOP 768 CD: Verona 27090-27091 CD: EMI CMS 764 9412 Excerpts LP: Melodram MEL 081
Milan 11 July 1958	Gencer, Bertocci, Clabassi RAI Milano Orchestra & Chorus Gavazzeni	LP: Ed Smith EJS 167 LP: Replica ARPL 32407 CD: Phoenix PX 5032 Excerpts CD: Memories HR 4386-4387/HR 4517-4518

la favorita

Mexico 12 July 1949	Role of Leonora Di Stefano, Mascherini, Siepi Bellas Artes Orchestra & Chorus Picco	LP: Cetra LO 2 LP: Ed Smith EJS 319 LP: Raritas 406 CD: Legato SRO 816
Milan 26 November 1952	Poggi, Silveri, Bruscantini RAI Milano Orchestra & Chorus Gavazzeni	Unpublished radio broadcast
Florence August 1955	Poggi, Bastianini, Hines Maggio musicale Orchestra & Chorus Erede	LP: Decca LXT 5146-5148/GOM 525-527/ GOS 525-527 LP: London SRS 63510 CD: Decca 452 4692 CD: Bramante CBCD 8029-8030 Excerpts 45: Decca CEP 575 LP: Decca GRV 16 CD: Decca 440 4062 CD: Grandi voci GVS 08
Naples 11 May 1963	Raimondi, Zanasi, Zaccaria San Carlo Orchestra & Chorus Previtali	CD: Bongiovanni GAO 105-106

la favorita, excerpt (pietoso al par del nume)

San Francisco 18 October 1953	Valletti San Francisco Opera Orchestra Cleva	LP: Voce 111
Forli 29 May 1957	Poggi Orchestra	CD: Bongiovanni GB 1097

MANUEL DE FALLA (1876-1946)

atlantida

Milan 18 June 1962	Stratas, Ganzarolli, Browne, Holley La Scala Orchestra & Chorus Schippers <u>Sung in Italian</u>	Unpublished radio broadcast

UMBERTO GIORDANO (1867-1948)

andrea chenier

Milan 1941	<u>Role of Contessa</u> Caniglia, Huder, Gigli, Bechi, Tajo, Taddei La Scala Orchestra & Chorus De Fabritiis	78: HMV DB 5423-5435 LP: HMV (Italy) QALP 10069-10070 LP: Victor LCT 6014 LP: World Records H 105-106 LP: Angel 6019 LP: EMI 3C153 17069-17070 CD: EMI CHS 769 9962

LUIGI GIORDIGIANI (1806-1860)

l'addio del pastore

18 December 1956	Bettarini	LP: Timaclub 77-78

CHRISTOPH WILLIBALD GLUCK (1714-1787)

orfeo ed euridice

Salzburg 5 August 1959	Role of Orfeo Jurinac, Sciutti Vienna Opera Chorus VPO Karajan	LP: Legendary LR 132 LP: Replica ARPL 22436 CD: Nuova era NE 2215-2216 CD: Memories HR 4382-4383 CD: DG 439 1012 Excerpts LP: Melodram MEL 081 CD: Memories HR 4386-4387

PIETRO MASCAGNI (1863-1945)

cavalleria rusticana

Milan 1940	Role of Lucia Rasa, Gigli, Bechi La Scala Orchestra & Chorus Mascagni	78: HMV DB 3960-3970 LP: HMV ALP 1610-1612 LP: HMV (Italy) QALP 108-109 LP: Electrola E 80474-80475 LP: Victor LCT 6000 LP: Angel 6008 LP: EMI 3C153 17074-17075 CD: EMI CHS 769 9872 Excerpts LP: Electrola E 80594
Mexico 13-18 June 1950	Role of Santuzza Filippeschi, Morelli Bellas Artes Orchestra & Chorus Mugnai	Unpublished radio broadcast
Turin 1952	Braschi, Tagliabue RAI Torino Orchestra & Chorus Basile	LP: Cetra LPC 1233/LPS 3233 CD: Cetra CDO 27 Excerpts LP: Cetra LPC 50144/LPC 55046/LEC 36 CD: Grandi voci GVS 08
Milan 10 May 1955	Di Stefano, Guelfi La Scala Orchestra & Chorus Votto	LP: Ed Smith UORC 259 LP: MRF Records MRF 142 LP: Cetra LO 15 CD: Di Stefano GDS 1001 CD: Myto MCD 981180
New York 16 November 1959	Björling, Cassel Metropolitan Opera Orchestra & Chorus Verchi	LP: Historical Recording Enterprises HRE 301 Excerpts LP: Ed Smith EJS 530

cavalleria rusticana/concluded

Rome
June
1960
	Del Monaco,
	MacNeil
	Santa Cecilia
	Orchestra & Chorus
	Serafin
		LP: Decca LXT 5613-5615/LXT 5643-5644/
		    SXL 2253-2255/SXL 2281-2282/
		    GOM 588-589/GOS 588-589
		LP: London OSA 1213
		CD: Decca 421 8072
		Excerpts
		45: Decca CEP 659/CEP 712/SEC 5103
		LP: Decca LXT 6012/SXL 6012/GRV 16

Tokyo 21 October 1961	Lo Forese, D'Orazi NHK Orchestra and Chorus Morelli	CD: Gala GL 100.518 CD: Rodolphe RPC 32755/RPV 32693-32694
Milan 7 December 1963	Corelli, Guelfi La Scala Orchestra & Chorus Gavazzeni	LP: Morgan MOR 6301 LP: Historical Recording Enterprises HRE 413 LP: Cetra DOC 58 CD: Arkadia CD 564/CDHP 564

cavalleria rusticana, excerpt (voi lo sapete)

Chicago 10 November 1956	Lyric Opera Orchestra Solti	LP: Decca LXT 5326

zanetto

Milan 10 May 1955	Role of Zanetto Carteri La Scala Orchestra & Chorus Votto	LP: MRF Records MRF 81

SALZBURGER FESTSPIELE 1957

FALSTAFF

(IN ITALIENISCHER SPRACHE)

KOMISCHE OPER IN DREI AKTEN VON ARRIGO BOITO

MUSIK VON
GIUSEPPE VERDI

MUSIKALISCHE UND SZENISCHE LEITUNG:
HERBERT VON KARAJAN

BÜHNENBILD UND KOSTÜME:
G. BARTOLINI-SALIMBENI

ORCHESTER
DIE WIENER PHILHARMONIKER
CHOR UND BALLETT DER WIENER STAATSOPER

FALSTAFF
(In italienischer Sprache)
Komische Oper in drei Akten von Arrigo Boito
MUSIK VON GIUSEPPE VERDI

Sir John Falstaff	Tito Gobbi
Ford, Alicens Mann	Rolando Panerai
Fenton	Giuseppe Zampieri
Dr. Cajus	Tomaso Spataro
Bardolf | in Falstaffs Diensten	Renato Ercolani
Pistol	Mario Petri
Mrs. Alice Ford	Elisabeth Schwarzkopf
Nanette, deren Tochter	Anna Moffo
Mrs. Meg Page	Anna Maria Canali
Mrs. Quickly	Giulietta Simionato

Bürger und Volk, Diener Fords, Maskenfiguren,
Kobolde, Feen usw.
Zeit: Während der Regierung Heinrich IV.
Schauplatz: Windsor
In der Dekoration und den Kostümen der Mailänder Scala

Pause nach dem zweiten und vierten Bild

Der offizielle Almanach „Salzburg — Festspiele 1957" ist auch für Sie der unentbehrliche Ratgeber
The official almanac "Salzburg Festivals 1957" is an indispensable guide for all Festival visitors
L'almanach officiel «Salzbourg Festival 1957» est indispensable à tous ceux qui s'intéressent au Festival

JULES MASSENET (1842-1912)

werther

Mexico 26 July 1949	Role of Charlotte Di Stefano, Rocabruna Bellas Artes Orchestra & Chorus Cellini Sung in Italian	LP: Ed Smith EJS 547 LP: ERR 111 LP: Cetra LO 30 Excerpts LP: Ed Smith EJS 303
Milan 21 April 1951	Tagliavini, Orlandini La Scala Orchestra & Chorus Capuana Sung in Italian	Unpublished radio broadcast Excerpts LP: Timaclub 77-78

werther, excerpt (air des lettres)

Milan 20 April 1951	Milan SO Quadri Sung in Italian	78: HMV (Italy) GQX 11499 LP: EMI 3C053 18031/EX 769 7411 CD: EMI CHS 769 7412 CD: Grandi voci GVS 08
Milan 20 December 1954	RAI Milano Orchestra Argento Sung in Italian	LP: Voci celebri MPV 5 LP: Cetra LMR 5006 CD: Cetra CDMR 5006
Rome July 1956	Santa Cecilia Orchestra Previtali	LP: Decca LXT 5458 CD: Decca 440 4062

werther, excerpt (qui m'aurait dit la place?)

Milan 4 May 1951	Milan SO Quadri Sung in Italian	78: Columbia (Italy) GQX 11499 LP: EMI 3C053 18031 CD: Grandi voci GVS 08

GIAN CARLO MENOTTI (Born 1911)

amahl and the night visitors

Florence 9 May 1953	Role of Mother Corena, Cordova, Lazzari Maggio musicale Orchestra & Chorus Stokowski	Unpublished radio broadcast

GIACOMO MEYERBEER (1791-1864)

les huguenots

Milan
28 May
1962

Role of Valentine
Sutherland,
Cossotto,
Corelli, Ghiaurov,
Ganzarolli
La Scala
Orchestra & Chorus
Gavazzeni
Sung in Italian

LP: Morgan MOR 6202
LP: Ed Smith EJS 246
LP: MRF Records MRF 18
LP: Hope Records HOPE 248
LP: Cetra DOC 34
LP: Great Opera Performances GOP 2
CD: Great Opera Performances GOP 701
CD: Melodram CDM 37026
CD: Gala GL 100.604
Excerpts
CD: Melodram MEL 16503
CD: Memories HR 4386-4387

CLAUDIO MONTEVERDI (1567-1643)

il combattimento di tancredi e clorinda, cantata

Naples
12 April
1952

Rovero, Valletti
San Carlo
Orchestra
Sanzogno

LP: Ed Smith EJS 453
LP: Historical Recording Enterprises
    HRE 301

WOLFGANG AMADEUS MOZART (1756-1791)

la clemenza di tito

Milan 24 January 1966	<u>Role of Servilia</u> Alva, Gordoni, Morelli Piccolo Scala Orchestra & Chorus Sanzogno	Unpublished radio broadcast <u>Simionato's final stage appearances</u>

così fan tutte

Geneva 14 January 1949	<u>Role of Dorabella</u> Danco, Morel, De Lucia, Cortis, Stabile Grand Théatre Orchestra & Chorus Böhm	LP: Rodolphe RPP 12456-12458

le nozze di figaro

Naples 24 February 1954	<u>Role of Cherubino</u> Tebaldi, Noni, Tajo, Colombo San Carlo Orchestra & Chorus Perlea	Unpublished radio broadcast

le nozze di figaro, excerpt (voi che sapete)

Chicago 10 November 1956	Lyric Opera Orchestra Solti	LP: Decca LXT 5326
Turin 30 December 1957	RAI Torino Orchestra La Rosa Parodi	LP: Timaclub 77-78

le nozze di figaro, excerpt (non so più)

San Francisco 18 October 1953	San Francisco Opera Orchestra Cleva	LP: Voce 111
Turin 30 December 1957	RAI Torino Orchestra La Rosa Parodi	LP: Timaclub 77-78

NEGLIA

il saluto di beatrice; come quel fior

December 1946 Bossi LP: Timaclub 77-78

FERDINANDO PAER (1771-1839)

il bacio della partenza

18 December 1956 Bettarini LP: Timaclub 77-78

AMILCARE PONCHIELLI (1834-1886)

la gioconda

Florence July 1957	Role of Laura Cerquetti, Del Monaco, Bastianini, Siepi Maggio musicale Orchestra & Chorus Gavazzeni	LP: Decca LXT 5400-5402/SXL 2225-2227/ GOM 609-611/GOS 699-611 LP: London SRS 63518 CD: Decca 433 7702 Excerpts 45: Decca CEP 584 LP: Decca SXL 2213/BR 3028

la gioconda, excerpt (è un anatema!/l'amo comè il fulgor)

Chicago 10 November 1956	Tebaldi Lyric Opera Orchestra Solti	LP: Decca LXT 5326 CD: Great Opera Performances GOP 721 CD: Decca 448 1542/455 2952

GIACOMO PUCCINI (1858-1924)

suor angelica

Florence 12-26 July 1962	Role of La Zia Tebaldi Maggio musicale Orchestra & Chorus Gardelli	LP: Decca LXT 6123/MET 236-238/ SXL 6123/SET 236-238 LP: London A 4152/OSA 1152/OSA 1364 CD: Decca 411 6652

GIOACHINO ROSSINI (1792-1868)

il barbiere di siviglia

Mexico 7 July 1949	Role of Rosina Di Stefano, Mascherini, Siepi Bellas Artes Orchestra & Chorus Cellini	CD: Di Stefano GDS 1052 Excerpts LP: Ed Smith EJS 302
Milan 1950	Infantino, Taddei, Badioli RAI Milano Orchestra & Chorus Previtali	LP: Cetra LPC 1211/LPS 3211 LP: DG LPM 18 170-18 172 CD: Cetra CDO 6 Excerpts LP: Cetra LPC 50140/LPC 55059/LEC 36 CD: Grandi voci GVS 08
Florence 3-12 September 1956	Misciano, Basianini, Corena, Siepi Maggio musicale Orchestra & Chorus Erede	LP: Decca LXT 5283-5285/ECS 611-613/D38 D3 LP: London RS 63011 CD: Decca 443 5362 Excerpts 45: Decca CEP 505 LP: Decca LXT 5480/BR 3088/GRV 16 CD: Decca 458 6532
Tokyo 23 October 1963	Sabatucci, Protti, Rossi-Lemeni NHK Orchestra and Chorus De Fabritiis	Unpublished radio broadcast

il barbiere di siviglia, excerpt (una voce poco fa)

Rome July- August 1954	Santa Cecilia Orchestra Ghione	LP: Decca LW 5139/LXT 5458 CD: Decca 440 4062
Milan 26 November 1956	RAI Milano Orchestra Sanzogno	LP: Cetra LMR 5015

la cenerentola

Turin 1950	Role of Angelina Valletti, Rovero, Meletti RAI Torino Orchestra & Chorus Rossi	LP: Cetra LPC 1208/LPS 3208/LPO 2017 LP: Everest S 423 CD: Cetra CDO 34 Excerpts LP: Cetra LEC 36
Naples 12 December 1953	Oncina, Taddei, Tajo San Carlo Orchestra & Chorus Serafin	Unpublished radio broadcast
Florence July- August 1963	Benelli, Bruscantini, Montarsolo Maggio musicale Orchestra & Chorus De Fabritiis	LP: Decca MET 265-267/SET 265-267/ GOM 631-633/GOS 631-633 LP: London OSA 1376 CD: Decca 433 0302 Excerpts LP: Decca GRV 16 CD: Grandi voci GVS 08

la cenerentola, excerpt (nacqui all' affanno)

Den Haag 30 June 1954	La Scala Chorus Residentie Orchestra Giulini	CD: Globe GL 6900/GLO 6901
Rome July- August 1954	Santa Cecilia Orchestra Ghione	LP: Decca LW 5139/LXT 5458 CD: Decca 440 4062
Milan 26 November 1956	RAI Milano Orchestra Sanzogno	LP: Cetra LMR 5015 CD: Memories HR 4386-4387/HR 4419-4420

l'italiana in algeri

Milan 5-12 August 1954	Role of Isabella Sciutti, Valletti, Petri, Cortis La Scala Orchestra & Chorus Giulini	LP: Columbia 33CX 1215-1216 LP: Columbia (France) 33FCX 388-389 LP: Columbia (Italy) 33QCX 10111-10112 LP: Angel 3529/6119 LP: EMI 3C163 00981-00982/RLS 747 CD: EMI CHS 764 0412 Excerpts LP: EMI 3C053 18031

l'italiana in algeri, excerpt (pensa alla patria)

Milan 26 November 1956	RAI Milano Orchestra Sanzogno	LP: Cetra LMR 5015 CD: Memories HR 4386-4387

semiramide

Milan 19 December 1962	Role of Arsace Sutherland, Raimondi, Ganzarolli La Scala Orchestra & Chorus Santini	LP: Ed Smith EJS 259 LP: Cetra DOC 40 CD: Curcio OP 114

tancredi, excerpt (di tanti palpiti)

Milan 20 December 1954	RAI Milano Orchestra Argento	LP: Cetra LMR 5006 LP: Voci celebri MPV 5 CD: Cetra CDMR 5006
Milan 26 November 1956	RAI Milano Orchestra Sanzogno	LP: Ed Smith EJS 360 LP: Cetra LMR 5015 CD: Memories HR 4386-4387/HR 4419-4420

CAMILLE SAINT-SAENS (1835-1921)

samson et dalila

Atlanta 4 May 1965	Role of Dalila Usunow, Diaz, Mittelmann Metropolitan Opera Orchestra & Chorus Cleva	Unpublished private recording Metropolitan tour performance
Detroit 28 May 1965	Vickers, Diaz, Macurdy Metropolitan Opera Orchestra & Chorus Cleva	Unpublished private recording Metropolitan tour performance

samson et dalila, excerpt (mon coeur s'ouvre à ta voix)

San Francisco 18 October 1953	San Francisco Opera Orchestra Cleva Sung in Italian	LP: Voce 111
Chicago 10 November 1956	Lyric Opera Orchestra Solti	45: Decca CEP 569 LP: Decca LXT 5326 CD: Grandi voci GVS 08 CD: Decca 448 1542/455 2952

samson et dalila, excerpt (printemps qui commence)

Milan 8 May 1951	Milan SO Quadri Sung in Italian	78: Columbia (Italy) GQX 11488 LP: EMI 3C053 18031
Rome July 1956	Santa Cecilia Orchestra Previtali	LP: Decca LXT 5458 CD: Decca 440 4062

samson et dalila, excerpt (amour viens aider ma faiblesse)

Milan 8 May 1951	Milan SO Quadri Sung in Italian	78: Columbia (Italy) GQX 11488 LP: EMI 3C053 18031

SALZBURGER FESTSPIELE 1962

DRITTES ORCHESTERKONZERT

GIUSEPPE VERDI

REQUIEM

Dirigent
HERBERT VON KARAJAN

Solisten:
LEONTYNE PRICE
GIULIETTA SIMIONATO
GIUSEPPE ZAMPIERI
NICOLAI GJAUROFF

DAS BERLINER PHILHARMONISCHE ORCHESTER
DER SINGVEREIN DER GESELLSCHAFT DER MUSIKFREUNDE WIEN

DONNERSTAG, DEN 9. AUGUST 1962, 20.30 UHR
IM NEUEN FESTSPIELHAUS

DRITTES ORCHESTERKONZERT

GIUSEPPE VERDI
REQUIEM

1. Requiem
2. Dies irae
3. Offertorium
4. Sanctus
5. Agnus Dei
6. Lux aeterna
7. Libera me

Choreinstudierung: Reinhold Schmid

Der offizielle Almanach „Salzburg — Festspiele 1962" ist auch für Sie der unentbehrliche Ratgeber
The official almanac "Salzburg Festivals 1962" is an indispensable guide for all Festival visitors
L'almanach officiel «Salzbourg Festival 1962» est indispensable à tous ceux qui s'intéressent au Festival

AMBROISE THOMAS (1811-1896)

mignon

Mexico 28 June 1949	Role of Mignon Di Stefano, Siepi, Ruffino Bellas Artes Orchestra & Chorus Mugnai Sung in Italian	LP: ERR 112 Excerpts LP: Ed Smith EJS 302 CD: Bongiovanni GAO 128-129

mignon, excerpt (connais-tu le pays?)

Milan 14 March 1949	Milan SO Quadri Sung in Italian	78: Columbia (Italy) GQ 7235 LP: EMI 3C053 18031 LP: Timaclub 77-78
Rome July 1956	Santa Cecilia Orchestra Previtali	LP: Decca LXT 5458 CD: Decca 440 4062

mignon, excerpt (je connais un pauvre enfant)

Milan 14 March 1949	Milan SO Quadri Sung in Italian	78: Columbia (Italy) GQX 11503 LP: EMI 3C053 18031
Milan 20 December 1954	RAI Milano Orchestra Argento Sung in Italian	LP: Cetra LMR 5006 LP: Voci celebri MPV 5 CD: Grandi voci GVS 08 CD: Cetra CDMR 5006
Turin 30 December 1957	RAI Torino Orchestra La Rosa Parodi Sung in Italian	LP: Timaclub 77-78

GIUSEPPE VERDI (1813-1901)

requiem

Salzburg 9 August 1962	L.Price, Zampieri, Ghiaurov Wiener Singverein BPO Karajan	Unpublished radio broadcast

aida

Mexico 30 May 1950	Role of Amneris Callas, Baum, Weede, Moscona Bellas Artes Orchestra & Chorus Picco	LP: Ed Smith UORC 200 LP: Historical Recording Enterprises CD: Melodram MEL 26009
Rome 1951	Mancini, Filippeschi, Panerai, Neri RAI Roma Orchestra & Chorus Gui	LP: Cetra LPS 1228 LP: DG LPM 18 173-18 175 Excerpts 45: DG EPL 30134/EPL 30136 LP: Cetra LEC 36 CD: Grandi voci GVS 08
London 4 June 1953	Callas, Baum, Walters, Neri Covent Garden Orchestra & Chorus Barbirolli	CD: Legato LCD 187 Excerpts LP: FWR 646 LP: Robin Hood RHR 500 CD: Eklipse EKRCD 14 CD: Melodram MEL 36513
Milan 7 December 1956	Stella, Di Stefano, Guelfi La Scala Orchestra & Chorus Votto	LP: Ed Smith UORC 317 LP: Di Stefano GDS 1003 LP: Paragon DSV 52026 LP: Replica ARPL 32448 CD: Legato LCD 204
Vienna 2-15 September 1959	Tebaldi, Bergonzi, MacNeil, Van Mill Wiener Singverein VPO Karajan	LP: Decca LXT 5539-5541/SXL 2167-2169 LP: London OSA 1313 CD: Decca 414 0872 Excerpts 45: Decca SEC 5075 LP: Decca LXT 5597/SXL 2242/GRV 16

aida/continued

Milan 21 April 1960	Nilsson, Ferraro, MacNeil, Ghiaurov La Scala Orchestra & Chorus Sanzogno	Unpublished radio broadcast
Tokyo 16 October 1961	Tucci, Del Monaco, Protti NHK Orchestra and Chorus Capuana	CD: Gala GL 100.507 Excerpts LP: Legendary LR 185
New York 1 December 1962	Tucci, Konya, Merrill, Siepi Metropolitan Opera Orchestra & Chorus Santi	Unpublished Met broadcast
Vienna 3 June 1963	L.Price, Usunow, Bastianini, Kreppel Vienna Opera Chorus VPO Matacic	LP: Melodram MEL 410 LP: Foyer FO 1036 CD: Foyer 2CF-2018 Excerpts CD: Memories HR 4386-4387/HR 4396-4397
London 4 February 1964	Vishnevskaya, Vickers, Glossop, Rouleau Covent Garden Orchestra & Chorus Balkwill	Unpublished radio broadcast
Cleveland 1 May 1965	Curtis-Verna, Corelli, Guarrera Metropolitan Opera Orchestra & Chorus Adler	Unpublished private recording Metropolitan tour performance

aida, excerpts (alta cagion v'aduna...to end scene 1; fu la sortè; pace t'imploro!)

Mexico 3 June 1950	Callas, Baum, Weede Bellas Artes Orchestra & Chorus Picco	LP: Opera Dubs OD 101-102 CD: Eklipse EKRCD 44

un ballo in maschera

Milan 7 December 1957	Role of Ulrica Callas, Ratti, Di Stefano, Bastianini La Scala Orchestra & Chorus Gavazzeni	LP: Morgan MOR 5709 LP: MRF Records MRF 83 LP: BJR Records BJR 127 LP: Cetra LO 55 LP: Replica ARPL 32445 CD: Great Opera Performances GOP 13 CD: Arkadia CD 519/CDHP 519 CD: Virtuoso 269.7412
Rome July 1961	Nilsson, Stahlman, Bergonzi, MacNeil Santa Cecilia Orchestra & Chorus Solti	LP: Decca LXT 2034-2036/MET 215-217/ SXL 2034-2036/SET 215-217 LP: London OSA 1328 Excerpts LP: Decca LXT 6013/SXL 6013/GRV 16 CD: Decca 440 4062 CD: Grandi voci GVS 08

don carlo

Salzburg 26 July 1958	Role of Eboli Jurinac, Fernandi, Bastianini, Siepi Vienna Opera Chorus VPO Karajan	LP: ERR 119 LP: Cetra LO 72 LP: Foyer FO 1029 LP: Dei della musica DMV 31-33 CD: Arkadia CDKAR 220 CD: DG 447 6552 Excerpts LP: Melodram MEL 081
Chicago 14 October 1960	Roberti, Tucker, Gobbi, Christoff Lyric Opera Orchestra & Chorus Votto	LP: Edizione lirica EL 014 LP: Stradivarius STR 1026 CD: Great Opera Performances GOP 38
Vienna 23 September 1961	Stella, Labò, Wächter, Kreppel Vienna Opera Chorus VPO Cleva	Unpublished radio broadcast

don carlo, excerpt (o don fatale)

Rome July- August 1954	Santa Cecilia Orchestra Ghione	45: Decca 45-71094 LP: Decca LW 5139/LXT 5458/GRV 16 CD: Decca 440 4062 CD: Grandi voci GVS 08

falstaff

Salzburg 10 August 1957	Role of Quickly Schwarzkopf, Moffo, Canali, Alva, Gobbi, Panerai Vienna Opera Chorus VPO Karajan	CD: Arkadia CDKAR 226
Chicago 10 October 1958	Tebaldi, Moffo, Misciano, Gobbi, MacNeil Lyric Opera Orchestra & Chorus Serafin	LP: Historical Recording Enterprises CD: Legato LCD 206
Rome 6-18 July 1964	Ligabue, Freni, Elias, Kraus, Evans, Merrill RCA Italiana Orchestra & Chorus Solti	LP: Victor LM 6163/LSC 6163/ SER 5509-5511 LP: Decca 2BB 104-106 LP: London OSA 1395 CD: Decca 417 1682

la forza del destino

Rio 2 September 1954	Role of Preziosilla Tebaldi, Penno, Silveri, Neri Orchestra & Chorus De Fabritiis	Unpublished radio broadcast
Rome July 1955	Tebaldi, Del Monaco, Bastianini, Siepi, Corena Santa Cecilia Orchestra & Chorus Molinari-Pradelli	LP: Decca LXT 5131-5134/SXL 2069-2072/ · GOM 597-599/GOS 597-599 LP: London OSA 1405 CD: Decca 421 5982 Excerpts 45: Decca CEP 644/SEC 5054 LP: Decca GRV 16 CD: Decca 440 4062
Rome 28 September 1957	Cerquetti, Ferraro, Protti, Christoff, Capecchi RAI Roma Orchestra & Chorus Sanzogno	LP: Ed Smith UORC 332 LP: Replica ARPL 32499 CD: Bongiovanni GAO 174-176
Vienna 23 September 1960	Stella, Di Stefano, Bastianini, Kreppel, Dönch Vienna Opera Chorus VPO Mitropoulos	LP: Morgan 6002 LP: Melodram MEL 023 CD: Di Stefano GDS 31022
Milan 7 December 1965	Ligabue, Bergonzi, Cappuccilli/ Meliciani, Christoff, Capecchi La Scala Orchestra & Chorus Gavazzeni	Unpublished radio broadcast

rigoletto

Rome July 1954	Role of Maddalena Güden, Del Monaco, Protti, Siepi Santa Cecilia Orchestra & Chorus Erede	LP: Decca LXT 5006-5008/ACL 203-205/ ECS 215-217 CD: Decca 440 2422 Excerpts 45: Decca 45-71081 LP: Decca LW 5206/LXT 5397

il trovatore

Mexico 20 June 1950	Role of Azucena Callas, Baum, Warren, Moscona Bellas Artes Orchestra & Chorus Picco	LP: Historical Recording Enterprises HRE 207 CD: Melodram MEL 26017/GM 20015

Geneva
20-26
June
1956
	Tebaldi,
	Del Monaco,
	Savarese, Tozzi
	Grand Théatre
	Orchestra & Chorus
	Erede
		LP: Decca LXT 5260-5262/SXL 2129-2131/
		    GOM 614-616/GOS 614-616
		CD: Decca 411 8742
		Excerpts
		45: Decca CEP 659
		LP: Decca LXT 5643-5644/SXL 2281-2282/
		    BR 3024/GRV 16
		CD: Decca 440 4062
		CD: Grandi voci GVS 08

New York 27 February 1960	Stella, Bergonzi, Bastianini, Wildermann Metropolitan Opera Orchestra & Chorus Cleva	LP: Great Opera Performances GFC 005
Salzburg 31 July 1962	L.Price, Corelli, Bastianini Vienna Opera Chorus VPO Karajan	LP: Morgan MOR 6201 LP: Hope Records HOPE 247 LP: Historical Recording Enterprises HRE 287 LP: Melodram MEL 710 LP: Arkadia ARK 7 CD: Movimento musica 03.018 CD: Rodolophe RPP 32482 CD: DG 447 6592 Excerpts CD: Memories HR 4386-4387

il trovatore/continued

Salzburg 13 August 1963	L.Price, McCracken, Bastianini Vienna Opera Chorus VPO Karajan	Unpublished radio broadcast
Tokyo 16 October 1963	Stella, Limarilli, Bastianini NHK Orchestra and Chorus De Fabritiis	CD: Rodolphe RPP 32752

Rome
July-
August
1964
	Tucci, Corelli,
	Merrill
	Rome Opera
	Orchestra & Chorus
	Schippers
		LP: EMI AN 151-153/SAN 151-153/SLS 916/
		    SMA 91406-91408/3C165 00042-00044
		LP: Angel 3653
		CD: EMI CMS 763 6402
		Excerpts
		LP: EMI ASD 2395/3C053 18031/
		    3C065 01704/SHZE 145
		CD: EMI CDM 763 4662

Moscow 10 September 1964	Tucci, Bergonzi Cappuccilli La Scala Orchestra & Chorus Gavazzeni	LP: Historical Recording Enterprises CD: Phoenix PHE 6621 CD: Melodram CDM 27008 Excerpts CD: Legato LCD 147
London 26 November 1964	Jones, Prevedi, Glossop, Rouleau Covent Garden Orchestra & Chorus Giulini	LP: Legendary LR 175

214 Simionato

MISCELLANEOUS

te voglio bene asaje, attributed to donizetti

Date not confirmed   LP: Ed Smith EJS 452

Elisabeth Höngen
1906-1997

JOHANN SEBASTIAN BACH (1685-1750)

cantata no 170 "vergnügte ruh' beliebte seelenlust"

Munich	Bavarian State	LP: DG APM 14 028
24-26	Orchestra	LP: Decca (USA) DL 9682
October	Lehmann	CD: DG 457 9732
1951		

LUDWIG VAN BEETHOVEN (1770-1827)

symphony no 9 "choral"

Dresden March 1941	Teschemacher, Ralf, Herrmann Dresden Staatskapelle and Opera Chorus Böhm	78: Electrola DB 5652-5660 LP: EMI 1C137 53508-53513M
Berlin 22-24 March 1942	Briem, Anders, Watzke Kittel Choir BPO Furtwängler	LP: Melodiya D 010851-010854/M10 10851 009 LP: Unicorn UNI 100-101 LP: Turnabout TV4346-4347/TV4353-4354 LP: French Furtwängler Society SWF 7003-7004 LP: Everest SDBR 3241 LP: EMI 3C153 53810-53816M LP: Movieplay (Spain) 11.0090-11.0091 CD: Priceless D 13256 CD: French Furtwängler Society SWF 891 CD: Music and Arts CD 653 CD: Arkadia CDWFE 357 CD: Melodiya MEL 10 00715 CD: Documents LV 919-920 CD: Grammofono AB 78581 CD: Iron Needle IN 1348-1350 CD: Tahra FURT 1004-1007
Vienna 3 November- 14 December 1947	Schwarzkopf, Patzak, Hotter Wiener Singverein VPO Karajan	78: Columbia LX 1097-1105/LX 8612-8620 78: Columbia (France) LFX 846-854 78: Columbia (Austria) LVX 32-40 78: Columbia (Italy) GQX 11250-11258 LP: Toshiba EAC 30101 LP: EMI RLS 7714/2C153 03200-03205M CD: EMI CDH 761 0762 <u>Soloists only present at sessions</u> <u>10-14 December</u>

choral symphony/continued

Bayreuth
29 July
1951
	Schwarzkopf,
	Hopf, Edelmann
	Bayreuth Festival
	Orchestra & Chorus
	Furtwängler
		LP: HMV ALP 1286-1287
		LP: HMV (France) FALP 381-383/
		  FALP 30048-30049/COLH 78-79/
		  UVT 3048-3049
		LP: HMV (Italy) QALP 10116-10117
		LP: Electrola E 90115-90116/EBE 600 000/
		  WALP 1286-1287/STE 90115-90116/
		  SME 90115-90116/SMVP 8051-8052
		LP: Victor LM 6043
		LP: Angel 4003/6068
		LP: EMI 1C147 00811-00812/
		  2C153 00811-00812/3C153 00811-00812/
		  1C149 53432-53439M/
		  2C153 52540-52551/2C151 53678-53679/
		  RLS 727
		CD: EMI CDC 747 0812/CDH 769 0812/
		  CHS 763 6062/CDH 566 2182

Vienna 6-9 February 1956	Lipp, Patzak, Wiener Wiener Singverein VSO Horenstein	LP: Vox PL 10 000/GBY 10 000 LP: Turnabout TV 37074 CD: Tuxedo TUXCD 1083 CD: Allegretto ACD 8052 <u>Orchestra described as Vienna Pro Musica</u>

symphony no 9 "choral", final bars only

Berlin 19 April 1942	Berger, Rosvaenge, Watzke Kittel Choir BPO Furtwängler	Unpublished newsreel recording <u>Picture only: sound taken from 22-24</u> <u>March recording listed above</u>

gellert-lieder

Munich 9 January 1953	Raucheisen	78: DG LVM 72 399 LP: DG LPEM 19 068

220 Höngen

GEORGES BIZET (1838-1875)

carmen

Dresden 4-5 December 1942	Role of Carmen Weidlich, Ralf, Herrmann Dresden Staatskapelle and Opera Chorus Böhm Sung in German	LP: Acanta BB 21362 CD: Preiser 90152 Excerpts LP: Acanta 10.213625/72.221792

carmen, excerpt (l'amour est un oiseau rebelle)

Stuttgart 17 October 1952	Württembergisches Staatsorchester Leitner Sung in German	45: DG NL 32 145 LP: Preiser 1111 165 CD: DG 457 9732

carmen, excerpt (melons! coupons!)

Stuttgart 18 November 1952	Plümacher, Junker-Giesen Württembergisches Staatorchester Leitner Sung in German	DG unpublished

carmen, excerpt (nous avons en tête une affaire!)

Vienna 29 September 1944	Loose, Hittorff, Klein, Wernigk VPO Baltzer Sung in German	CD: Preiser 90246 Unpublished Telefunken recording

JOHANNES BRAHMS (1833-1897)

alto rhapsody

Berlin 4-5 June 1952	Berliner Liedtafel BPO Leitner	78: DG LVM 72 231 LP: DG LP 16 105/LPX 29 256 LP: Decca (USA) DL 4074 CD: DG 457 9732

liebeslieder-walzer

Vienna 15-16 November 1947	Seefried, Meyer-Welfing, Hotter Wührer, Nordberg	78: Columbia LX 1114-1117/LCX 118-121/ LX 8628-8631 auto 78: Columbia (Austria) LVX 55-58 LP: World Records SH 373 CD: EMI CDH 566 4252

zigeunerlieder

Munich 28-29 March 1954	Weissenborn	LP: DG LPE 17 024 CD: DG 457 9732

PETER CORNELIUS (1824-1874)

sonnenuntergang

Berlin 13 November 1942	Raucheisen	Unpublished radio broadcast

ANTONIN DVORAK (1841-1904)

gipsy melodies

Munich 29-30 March 1954	Weissenborn <u>Sung in German</u>	LP: DG LPE 17 024

UMBERTO GIORDANO (1867-1948)

andrea chenier

Vienna 26 June 1960	<u>Role of Contessa</u> Tebaldi, Konetzni, Corelli, Bastianini, Paskalis Vienna Opera Chorus VPO Matacic	LP: Morgan MOR 6003 CD: Cetra CDE 1017 CD: Fabbri OP 10

FRANZ JOSEF HAYDN (1732-1809)

mass no 11 "nelson"

Vienna 1951	Della Casa, Taubmann, London Akademiechor VSO Sternberg	LP: Haydn Society HSLP 2004 LP: Nixa HLP 2004
Vienna May 1955	Stich-Randall, Dermota, Guthrie Akademiechor Volksoper Orchestra Rossi	LP: Bach Guild VRS 470 LP: Amadeo PVL 7071/AVRS 6121/AVRS 19023

PAUL HINDEMITH (1895-1963)

requiem for those we love

Vienna 1950	Braun Vienna Opera Chorus VSO Hindemith Sung in German	LP: Vox PL 1760/PNLP 1760 CD: Tuxedo TUXCD 1061

ENGELBERT HUMPERDINCK (1854-1921)

hänsel und gretel

Vienna
18-26
March
1964
	Role of Witch
	Rothenberger,
	Seefried, Maikl,
	G.Hoffman, Berry
	Wiener
	Sängerknaben
	VPO
	Cluytens
		LP: Electrola E 91366-91367/
		    STE 91366-91367/WALP 922-923/
		    ASDW 9152-9153
		LP: Angel 3648/6124
		LP: EMI 1C163 00792-00793
		CD: EMI CMS 565 6612
		Excerpts
		LP: Electrola E 80865/SME 80865
		LP: EMI 1C037 00751

FRANZ LISZT (1811-1886)

songs: es muss ein wunderbares sein; nimm' einen strahl der sonne

Vienna 3 February 1949	Nordberg	Columbia unpublished

CLAUDIO MONTEVERDI (1567-1643)

l'arianna, excerpt (lasciatemi morir, arranged by orff)

Stuttgart 19 November 1952	Graeser, double-bass Leitner and Reinhardt, harpsichords	45: DG EPA 37 011 LP: DG APM 14 020 CD: DG 457 9732
Stuttgart 19 November 1952	Württembergisches Staatsorchester Leitner <u>Sung in German</u>	DG unpublished

WOLFGANG AMADEUS MOZART (1756-1791)

requiem

Vienna 10-13 February 1956	Lipp, Dickie, Weber Wiener Singverein VSO Horenstein	LP: Vox DL 270

le nozze di figaro

Vienna 17-31 June 1950

<u>Role of Marcellina</u>
Schwarzkopf,
Seefried,
Jurinac, Kunz,
London
Vienna
Opera Chorus
VPO
Karajan

78: Columbia (Germany) LWX 410-425
LP: Columbia 33CX 1007-1009
LP: Columbia (Germany) C 90294-90296/
    33WCX 1007-1009
LP: Columbia (France) 33FCX 174-176
LP: Columbia (Austria) 33VCX 503-505
LP: Columbia (Italy) 33QCX 10002-10003
LP: EMI 1C147 01751-01753M/
    1C197 54200-54208M
CD: EMI CMS 769 6392
<u>Excerpts</u>
LP: Columbia 33CX 1558
LP: Columbia (Germany) C 80531/33WSX 548
LP: Columbia (France) 33FCX 30170

STAATSOPER WIEN

Dienstag, den 23. November 1943
Im Abonnement II. Gruppe. Preise III

Die Frau ohne Schatten
Oper in drei Akten von Hugo v. Hofmannsthal
Musik von Richard Strauß

Musikalische Leitung: Karl Böhm   Inszenierung: Georg Hartmann a. G.
Bühnenbilder und Kostüme: Robert Kautsky

Der Kaiser	Torsten Ralf
Die Kaiserin	Hilde Konetzni
Die Amme	Elisabeth Höngen
Geisterbote	Herbert Alsen
Ein Hüter der Schwelle des Tempels	Emmy Loose
Stimme eines Jünglings	Wenko Wenkoff
Die Stimme des Falken	Else Böttcher
Eine Stimme von oben	Melanie Frutschnigg
Barak, der Färber	Josef Herrmann
Sein Weib	Else Schulz
Der Einäugige ⎫	Georg Monthy
Der Einarmige ⎬ des Färbers Brüder	Marjan Rus
Der Bucklige ⎭	William Wernigk
Kinder- und Solostimmen	Elisabeth Rutgers / Dora Komar-Somborn / Maria Schober / Marie Langhans / Edith Prießner / Emmy Loose / Jarmila Barton / Dora With / Melanie Frutschnigg
Die Stimmen der Wächter der Stadt	Alfred Poell / Tomislav Neralic / Roland Neumann

Kaiserliche Diener, fremde Kinder. Dienende, Geister, Geisterstimmen

Ort der Handlung: I. Aufzug: Auf einer Terrasse über den kaiserlichen Gärten. — Färberhaus. — II. Aufzug: Färberhaus. — Wald vor dem Pavillon des Falkners. — Färberhaus. — Wald vor dem Pavillon des Falkners. — Färberhaus. — III. Aufzug: Unterirdischer Kerker. — Geistertempel: Eingang. — Geistertempel: Inneres. — Landschaft im Geisterreich.

Technische Einrichtung: Ferdinand Jaschke

Nach dem ersten Akt eine kleinere, nach dem zweiten Akt eine größere Pause

Anfang 17 Uhr   Ende 21 Uhr

Das Publikum wird gebeten, sich vor Beginn der Vorstellung beim Erscheinen unserer verwundeten Frontsoldaten in der Mittelloge von den Plätzen zu erheben.

STAATSOPER
IM THEATER AN DER WIEN

Sonntag, den 30. Jänner 1955
Beschränkter Kartenverkauf

Die Meistersinger von Nürnberg

Oper in drei Aufzügen von Richard Wagner
Musikalische Leitung: Rudolf Moralt
Inszenierung: Rudolf Hartmann
Bühnenbilder und Kostüme: Robert Kautsky

Hans Sachs, Schuster	⎫	Karl Kamann
Veit Pogner, Goldschmied		Ludwig Hofmann
Kunz Vogelsang, Kürschner		Hugo Meyer-Welfing
Konrad Nachtigall, Spengler		Hans Schweiger
Sixtus Beckmesser, Stadtschreiber		Erich Kunz
Fritz Kothner, Bäcker	Meister-	Fritz Krenn
Balthasar Zorn, Zinngießer	singer	Erich Majkut
Ulrich Eißlinger, Würzkrämer		Hermann Gallos
Augustin Moser, Schneider		Erwin Nowaro
Hermann Ortel, Seifensieder		Harald Pröglhöf
Hans Schwarz, Strumpfwirker		Franz Bierbach
Hans Foltz, Kupferschmied	⎭	Alfred Muzzarelli

Walther v. Stolzing, ein junger Ritter aus Franken Rudolf Lustig a. G.
David, Sachsens Lehrbube . . . . Murray Dickie
Eva, Pogners Tochter . . . . Irmgard Seefried
Magdalena, Evas Amme . . . . Elisabeth Höngen
Ein Nachtwächter . . . . Harald Pröglhöf

Bürger und Frauen aller Zünfte, Gesellen, Lehrbuben, Mädchen, Volk

Schauplatz der Handlung: Nürnberg. Um die Mitte des 16. Jahrhunderts

Erster Aufzug: Im Innern der Katharinenkirche — Zweiter Aufzug: In den Straßen vor den Häusern Pogners und Sachsens — Dritter Aufzug: a) Sachsens Werkstatt, b) ein freier Wiesenplan an der Pegnitz

Nach jedem Aufzug eine größere Pause

Kasseneröffnung 16½ Uhr Anfang 17½ Uhr Ende etwa 22½ Uhr

228 Höngen

die zauberflöte

Salzburg 27 July 1949	Role of 3rd Lady Seefried, Lipp, Oravez, W.Ludwig, Schmitt-Walter, Greindl, Schöffler Vienna Opera Chorus VPO Furtwängler	LP: Ed Smith EJS 572 LP: Discocorp IGI 572 LP: Hope Records HOPE 208 CD: Arlecchino ARL 78-80 CD: Music and Arts CD 882
Salzburg 16 August 1950	Seefried, Lipp, Heusser, W.Ludwig, Kunz, Greindl, Schöffler Vienna Opera Chorus VPO Furtwängler	Unpublished radio broadcast Final secion of opera missing from recording

die zauberflöte, excerpt (nur stille, stille!...to end of opera)

Vienna 14-16 November 1944	Role of 2nd Lady Seefried, Loose, Konetzni, Nikolaidi, Dermota, Kunz, Schöffler Vienna Opera Chorus VPO Böhm	CD: Preiser 90249

GIOVANNI PERGOLESI (1710-1736)

stabat mater

Vienna	Stich-Randall	LP: Bach Guild VRS 549
May	Akademiechor	LP: Amadeo AVRS 6029
1955	Volksoper Orchestra	
	Rossi	

OTTO NICOLAI (1810-1849)

das treue mädchen, duet

| Berlin | Scheppan | Unpublished radio broadcast. |
| 1944 | Raucheisen | |

CAMILLE SAINT-SAENS (1835-1921)

samson et dalila, excerpts (printemps qui commence; mon coeur s'ouvre à ta voix)

Hamburg	Philharmonisches	78: DG LM 68 442
20 February	Staatsorchester	45: DG EPL 30 218
1950	Leitner	LP: Preiser 1111 165
	<u>Sung in German</u>	CD: DG 457 9732

Höngen

FRANZ SCHUBERT (1797-1828)

an den mond (füllest wieder busch und tal)

Berlin   Raucheisen   Unpublished radio broadcast
20 November
1942

fragment aus dem aischylos (so wird der mann, der sonder zwang gerecht ist)

Berlin   Raucheisen   Unpublished radio broadcast
13 November
1942

im walde (windes rauschen, gottes flügel)

Berlin   Raucheisen   Unpublished radio broadcast
1942

ROBERT SCHUMANN (1810-1856)

frauenliebe und -leben, song cycle

Hamburg 17 February 1950	Leitner	78: DG LVM 72 009-72 010 LP: DG LPEM 19 068 LP: Decca (USA) DL 9610 CD: DG 457 9732

spanisches liederspiel, selection

Vienna 22 November 1944	Seefried, Dermota, Alsen L.Ludwig	Unpublished radio broadcast

die kartenlegerin (schlief die mutter endlich ein)

Vienna 5 November 1946	Zipper	78: Columbia LB 62 78: Columbia (USA) 17588D LP: EMI RLS 154 7003 CD: EMI CZS 569 7432

an den abendstern, duet

Berlin 1944	Scheppan Raucheisen	Unpublished radio broadcast

RICHARD STRAUSS (1864-1949)

elektra

London 24-26 October 1947	<u>Role of Klytemnestra</u> Schlüter, Welitsch, Widdop, Schöffler BBC Chorus RPO Beecham	LP: Ed Smith UORC 171 LP: Beecham Society WSA 509-512 LP: Rococo 1005 LP: Arkadia ARK 9 LP: Melodram MEL 041 CD: Myto MCD 946117
New York 23 February 1952	Varnay, Wegner, Svanholm, Schöffler Metropolitan Opera Orchestra and Chorus Reiner	LP: Private Edition SJS 704-705 LP: Metropoloitan Opera MET 9 CD: Arlecchino ARL 20-22

elektra, excerpt (ich will nichts hören!)

Munich 2 August 1952	Goltz Bavarian State Orchestra Solti	LP: DG LPEM 19 038 LP: Decca (USA) DL 9723 CD: DG 457 9732

die frau ohne schatten

Vienna 29 November- 10 December 1955	Role of Amme Rysanek, Goltz, Hopf, Schöffler Weber Vienna Opera Chorus VPO Böhm	LP: Decca LXT 5180-5184/GOM 554-557/ GOS 554-557 CD: Decca 425 9812
Vienna 9 November 1955	Rysanek, Goltz, Hopf, Schöffler, Weber Vienna Opera Chorus VPO Böhm	Unpublished radio broadcast

die frau ohne schatten, excerpts (ist mein liebster dahin?; ach herrin, süsse herrin!; fischlein fünf; barak, ich hab' es nicht getan!)

Vienna 23 December 1943	Konetzni, Loose, Schulz, Ralf, Herrmann, Alsen Vienna Opera Chorus VPO Böhmm	CD: Koch 3-1455-2

234 Höngen

der rosenkavalier, excerpt (da geht er hin/ach du bist wieder da!)

Vienna	Konetzni	CD: Preiser 90246
29 September	VPO	<u>Unpublished Telefunken recording</u>
1944	Baltzer	

der rosenkavalier, excerpt (mir ist die ehre widerfahr'n)

Vienna	Loose	CD: Preiser 90246
July	VPO	<u>Unpublished Telefunken recording</u>
1944	Baltzer	

der rosenkavalier, excerpt (hab mir's gelobt)

Vienna	Konetzni, Loose	78: Telefunken (Austria) E 1008
July	VPO	CD: Preiser 90246
1944	Baltzer	

der rosenkavalier, excerpt (ist ein traum, kann nicht wirklich sein)

Dresden	Rethy	78: Electrola DB 5617
1940	Dresden Staatskapelle	LP: EMI 1C137 53514-53519M/EX 29 01313
	Böhm	CD: Preiser 89401

salome

London	<u>Role of Herodias</u>	CD: Legato LCD 211
30 September	Cebotari,	<u>Höngen speaks her role, presumably</u>
1947	Patzak,	<u>due to indisposition</u>
	Rothmüller	
	VPO	
	Krauss	
New York	Welitsch,	LP: Discocorp SID 724/IGI 293
19 January	Svanholm, Hotter	LP: Metropolitan Opera MET 9
1952	Metropolitan Opera Orchestra	CD: Myto MCD 952125
	Reiner	

GIUSEPPE VERDI (1813-1901)

requiem

Vienna 30 September- 1 October 1944	Seefried, Dermota, Alsen Vienna Opera Chorus VPO Böhm	Unpublished radio broadcast Recording incomplete
Munich 1 December 1950	Cunitz, W.Ludwig, Greindl Bavarian Radio Orchestra & Chorus Jochum	CD: Orfeo C195 892H

aida

Hamburg 1951	Role of Amneris Zadek, Rosvaenge, Metternich, Fehn NDR Orchestra and Chorus Schmidt-Isserstedt Sung in German	LP: Cetra Opera live

aida, excerpt (fu la sortè dell' armi!)

Stuttgart 2 April 1951	Kupper Württembergisches Staatsorchester and Chorus Leitner Sung in German	LP: DG LPM 18 009/LPEM 19 027

don carlo, excerpt (pietà! perdon!; o don fatale)

Vienna July- September 1944	Konetzni VPO Baltzer Sung in German	CD: Preiser 90175 O don fatale only CD: Preiser 90345 Unpublished Telefunken recordings

236 Höngen

macbeth

Vienna	Role of Lady	LP: Urania URLP 220
31 May-	Macbeth	LP: Acanta DE 23278
1 June	Ahlersmayer,	CD: Preiser 90175
1943	Witt, Alsen	Excerpts
	Vienna	LP: Acanta KBF 21488
	Opera Chorus	
	VPO	
	Böhm	
	Sung in German	

macbeth, excerpt (una macchia è qui tuttora)

Stuttgart	Plümacher, Grefe	LP: DG LPM 18 047/LPEM 19 029
4 April	Württembergisches	LP: Preiser 1111 165
1951	Staatsorchester	CD: DG 457 9732
	Leitner	
	Sung in German	

il trovatore, excerpt (condotta ell' era in ceppi/ai nostri monti)

Stuttgart	W.Ludwig	78: DG LVM 72 120
4-5	Württembergisches	LP: DG LPM 18 047/LPEM 19 029
April	Staatsorchester	LP: Preiser 1111 165
1951	Leitner	CD: DG 457 9732
	Sung in German	

RICHARD WAGNER (1813-1883)

götterdämmerung

Milan 4 April 1950	Role of Waltraute Flagstad, Konetzni, Lorenz, Herrmann, Weber La Scala Orchestra & Chorus Furtwängler	LP: Ed Smith EJS 538 LP: Discocorp RR 420 LP: Murray Hill 940 477 LP: Everest S 476 LP: Cetra CFE 101/FE 40 CD: Cetra CDC 28 CD: Arkadia CDWFE 301/CDWFE 351/ CDWFE 364 CD: Virtuoso 269.9112/269.9082 CD: Music and Arts CD 914
Bayreuth 4 August 1951	Varnay, Mödl, Schwarzkopf, Aldenhoff, Uhde, Weber, Pflanzl Bayreuth Festival Orchestra & Chorus Knappertsbusch	Decca unpublished

götterdämmerung, excerpt (seit er von dir geschieden)

Stuttgart 18 November 1952	Württembergisches Staatsorchester Leitner	LP: DG LPEM 19 042/2548 709/2700 703 LP: Preiser 1111 165 CD: DG 457 9732

die meistersinger von nürnberg, excerpt (selig wir die sonne)

Vienna July- September 1944	Konetzni, Petrak, Mörwald, Schöffler VPO Baltzer	78: Telefunken (Austria) E 1008

parsifal

Vienna 1 April 1961	Role of Kundry (except for Act 2 scene 2) C.Ludwig, Uhl, Hotter, Berry Vienna Opera Chorus VPO Karajan	CD: Arkadia CDKAR 219

das rheingold

Vienna 1948-1949	Role of Fricka Steingruber, Anday, Pölzer, Poell, Frantz, Vogel VSO Moralt	CD: Myto MCD 962144
Milan 4 March 1950	Wegener, Weth-Falke, Markwort, Frantz, Pernerstorfer, Weber La Scala Orchestra Furtwängler	LP: Ed Smith UORC 128 LP: Discocorp RR 420 LP: Murray Hill 940 477 LP: Everest S 473 LP: Cetra CFE 101/FE 37 CD: Cetra CDC 26 CD: Arkadia CDWFE 301/CDWFE 351 CD: Virtuoso 269.7282/269.9082 CD: Music and Arts CD 914
Bayreuth 1 August 1951	Brivkalne, Schwarzkopf, Windgassen, S.Björling, Pflanzl Bayreuth Festival Orchestra Knappertsbusch	Decca unpublished

siegfried

Milan 22 March 1950	Role of Erda Flagstad, Moor, Svanholm, Markwort, Weber, Herrmann, Pernerstorfer La Scala Orchestra Furtwängler	LP: Ed Smith UORC 123 LP: Discocorp RR 420 LP: Murray Hill 940 477 LP: Everest S 475 LP: Cetra CFE 101/FE 39 CD: Cetra CDC 27 CD: Arkadia CDWFE 301/CDWFE 351 CD: Virtuoso 269.9082/269.9092 CD: Music and Arts CD 914

tristan und isolde, excerpt (doch nun von tristan?)

London 31 March 1948	Flagstad Philharmonia Dobrowen	78: HMV DB 6748-6749 78: Victor M 1435 45: Victor WDM 1435 LP: Victor LM 1151 LP: Electrola E 60619/WDLP 643 LP: Angel 6158/60082 LP: EMI HQM 1138/1C147 01491-01492M/ EX 29 12273/29 10373 CD: EMI CDH 763 0302

die walküre

Milan 9 March 1950	Role of Fricka Flagstad, Konetzni, Treptow, Frantz, Weber La Scala Orchestra Furtwängler	LP: Ed Smith EJS 534 LP: Discocorp RR 420 LP: Murray Hill 940 477 LP: Everest S 474 LP: Cetra LO 86/CFE 101/FE 38 CD: Cetra CDC 15 CD: Arkadia CDWFE 301/CDWFE 351 CD: Virtuoso 269.9082/269.9102 CD: Music and Arts CD 914
Bayreuth 2 August 1951	Rysanek, Varnay, Treptow, S.Björling, Van Mill Bayreuth Festival Orchestra Knappertsbusch	Decca unpublished

der engel/wesendonk-lieder

Vienna 7 November 1947	Nordberg	Columbia unpublished
London 14 April 1948	Moore	78: Columbia LX 1282

stehe still/wesendonk-lieder

Vienna 7 November 1947	Nordberg	78: Columbia LX 1282

im treibhaus/wesendonk-lieder

Vienna 5-7 November 1947	Nordberg	Columbia unpublished
London 14 April 1948	Moore	78: Columbia LX 1590

träume/wesendonk-lieder

Vienna 7 November 1947	Nordberg	Columbia unpublished
London 14 April 1948	Moore	78: Columbia LX 1590

schmerzen/wesendonk-lieder

Vienna 7 November 1947	Nordberg	Columbia unpublished
London 14 April 1948	Moore	Columbia unpublished

HUGO WOLF (1860-1903)

auf eine christblume/mörike-lieder

Vienna 6 November 1946	Zipper	Columbia unpublished
London 10 October 1947	Moore	78: Columbia LB 140

die geister am mummelsee/mörike-lieder

Berlin 1943	Raucheisen	LP: Acanta 22.226379

kennst du das land?/mignon-lieder

Vienna 6 November 1946	Zipper	Columbia unpublished
London 10 October 1947	Moore	Columbia unpublished

nur wer die sehnsucht kennt/mignon-lieder

Vienna 5 November 1946	Zipper	78: Columbia LB 62 78: Columbia (USA) 17588D LP: EMI EX 769 7411 CD: EMI CHS 769 7412/CZS 569 7432

um mitternacht/mörike-lieder

Berlin 1943	Raucheisen	LP: Acanta 22.226379

wie glänzt der helle mond/alte weisen

Berlin 1944	Raucheisen	Unpublished radio broadcast

Thursday, September 18th, 1947

COSI FAN TUTTE

A Comic Opera in Two Acts

Libretto by Lorenzo da Ponte

German Version following the tradition and the original
by George Schumann

Music by Mozart

Conductor : Josef Krips

Producer : Oscar Fritz Schuh

Decor : Robert Kautsky

Costumes : Caspar Neher

Fiordiligi	Two sisters	IRMGARD SEEFRIED
Dorabella	Ladies of Ferrara	ELISABETH HOENGEN

Guglielmo, an Officer, in love with Fiordiligi .　　ERICH KUNZ

Ferrando, an Officer, in love with Dorabella　　ANTON DERMOTA

Despina, Maid to the sisters　.　.　EMMY LOOSE

Don Alfonso, an old Philosopher　　.　PAUL SCHOEFFLER

Choreography by Willy Franzl

Visit to London by Wiener Staatsoper

credits

Valuable help with the supply of
information or illustration material
for these discographies came from

Ray Burford, Sony Classical London
Richard Chlupaty, London
Syd Gray, Hove
Michael Gray, Alexandria VA
Ken Jagger, EMI Classics London
Alan Newcombe, DG Hamburg
Brian Pinder, Halifax
Tully Potter, Billericay
Alan Sanders, Richmond
Malcolm Walker, Harrow

Discographies by Travis & Emery:

Discographies by John Hunt.

1987: From Adam to Webern: the Recordings of von Karajan.

1991: 3 Italian Conductors and 7 Viennese Sopranos: 10 Discographies: Arturo Toscanini, Guido Cantelli, Carlo Maria Giulini, Elisabeth Schwarzkopf, Irmgard Seefried, Elisabeth Gruemmer, Sena Jurinac, Hilde Gueden, Lisa Della Casa, Rita Streich.

1992: Mid-Century Conductors and More Viennese Singers: 10 Discographies: Karl Boehm, Victor De Sabata, Hans Knappertsbusch, Tullio Serafin, Clemens Krauss, Anton Dermota, Leonie Rysanek, Eberhard Waechter, Maria Reining, Erich Kunz.

1993: More 20th Century Conductors: 7 Discographies: Eugen Jochum, Ferenc Fricsay, Carl Schuricht, Felix Weingartner, Josef Krips, Otto Klemperer, Erich Kleiber.

1994: Giants of the Keyboard: 6 Discographies: Wilhelm Kempff, Walter Gieseking, Edwin Fischer, Clara Haskil, Wilhelm Backhaus, Artur Schnabel.

1994: Six Wagnerian Sopranos: 6 Discographies: Frieda Leider, Kirsten Flagstad, Astrid Varnay, Martha Moedl, Birgit Nilsson, Gwyneth Jones.

1995: Musical Knights: 6 Discographies: Henry Wood, Thomas Beecham, Adrian Boult, John Barbirolli, Reginald Goodall, Malcolm Sargent.

1995: A Notable Quartet: 4 Discographies: Gundula Janowitz, Christa Ludwig, Nicolai Gedda, Dietrich Fischer-Dieskau.

1996: The Post-War German Tradition: 5 Discographies: Rudolf Kempe, Joseph Keilberth, Wolfgang Sawallisch, Rafael Kubelik, Andre Cluytens.

1996: Teachers and Pupils: 7 Discographies: Elisabeth Schwarzkopf, Maria Ivoguen, Maria Cebotari, Meta Seinemeyer, Ljuba Welitsch, Rita Streich, Erna Berger.

1996: Tenors in a Lyric Tradition: 3 Discographies: Peter Anders, Walther Ludwig, Fritz Wunderlich.

1997: The Lyric Baritone: 5 Discographies: Hans Reinmar, Gerhard Hüsch, Josef Metternich, Hermann Uhde, Eberhard Wächter.

1997: Hungarians in Exile: 3 Discographies: Fritz Reiner, Antal Dorati, George Szell.

1997: The Art of the Diva: 3 Discographies: Claudia Muzio, Maria Callas, Magda Olivero.

1997: Metropolitan Sopranos: 4 Discographies: Rosa Ponselle, Eleanor Steber, Zinka Milanov, Leontyne Price.

1997: Back From The Shadows: 4 Discographies: Willem Mengelberg, Dimitri Mitropoulos, Hermann Abendroth, Eduard Van Beinum.

1997: More Musical Knights: 4 Discographies: Hamilton Harty, Charles Mackerras, Simon Rattle, John Pritchard.

1998: Conductors On The Yellow Label: 8 Discographies: Fritz Lehmann, Ferdinand Leitner, Ferenc Fricsay, Eugen Jochum, Leopold Ludwig, Artur Rother, Franz Konwitschny, Igor Markevitch.

1998: More Giants of the Keyboard: 5 Discographies: Claudio Arrau, Gyorgy Cziffra, Vladimir Horowitz, Dinu Lipatti, Artur Rubinstein.

1998: Mezzo and Contraltos: 5 Discographies: Janet Baker, Margarete Klose, Kathleen Ferrier, Giulietta Simionato, Elisabeth Höngen.
1999: The Furtwängler Sound Sixth Edition: Discography and Concert Listing.
1999: The Great Dictators: 3 Discographies: Evgeny Mravinsky, Artur Rodzinski, Sergiu Celibidache.
1999: Sviatoslav Richter: Pianist of the Century: Discography.
2000: Philharmonic Autocrat 1: Discography of: Herbert Von Karajan [Third Edition].
2000: Wiener Philharmoniker 1 - Vienna Philharmonic & Vienna State Opera Orchestras: Disc. Part 1 1905-1954.
2000: Wiener Philharmoniker 2 - Vienna Philharmonic & Vienna State Opera Orchestras: Disc. Part 2 1954-1989.
2001: Gramophone Stalwarts: 3 Separate Discographies: Bruno Walter, Erich Leinsdorf, Georg Solti.
2001: Singers of the Third Reich: 5 Discographies: Helge Roswaenge, Tiana Lemnitz, Franz Völker, Maria Müller, Max Lorenz.
2001: Philharmonic Autocrat 2: Concert Register of Herbert Von Karajan Second Edition.
2002: Sächsische Staatskapelle Dresden: Complete Discography.
2002: Carlo Maria Giulini: Discography and Concert Register.
2002: Pianists For The Connoisseur: 6 Discographies: Arturo Benedetti Michelangeli, Alfred Cortot, Alexis Weissenberg, Clifford Curzon, Solomon, Elly Ney.
2003: Singers on the Yellow Label: 7 Discographies: Maria Stader, Elfriede Trötschel, Annelies Kupper, Wolfgang Windgassen, Ernst Häfliger, Josef Greindl, Kim Borg.
2003: A Gallic Trio: 3 Discographies: Charles Münch, Paul Paray, Pierre Monteux.
2004: Antal Dorati 1906-1988: Discography and Concert Register.
2004: Columbia 33CX Label Discography.
2004: Great Violinists: 3 Discographies: David Oistrakh, Wolfgang Schneiderhan, Arthur Grumiaux.
2006: Leopold Stokowski: Second Edition of the Discography.
2006: Wagner Im Festspielhaus: Discography of the Bayreuth Festival.
2006: Her Master's Voice: Concert Register and Discography of Dame Elisabeth Schwarzkopf [Third Edition].
2007: Hans Knappertsbusch: Kna: Concert Register and Discography of Hans Knappertsbusch, 1888-1965. Second Edition.
2008: Philips Minigroove: Second Extended Version of the European Discography.
2009: American Classics: The Discographies of Leonard Bernstein and Eugene Ormandy.

Discography by Stephen J. Pettitt, edited by John Hunt:
1987: Philharmonia Orchestra: Complete Discography 1945-1987

Available from: Travis & Emery at 17 Cecil Court, London, UK. (+44) 20 7 240 2129. email on sales@travis-and-emery.com .

© Travis & Emery 2009

Music and Books published by Travis & Emery Music Bookshop:

Anon.: Hymnarium Sarisburense, cum Rubris et Notis Musicus
Agricola, Johann Friedrich from Tosi: Anleitung zur Singkunst. (Faksimile 1757)
Bach, C.P.E.: edited W. Emery: Nekrolog or Obituary Notice of J.S. Bach.
Bateson, Naomi Judith: Alcock of Salisbury
Bathe, William: A Briefe Introduction to the Skill of Song
Bax, Arnold: Symphony #5, Arranged for Piano Four Hands by Walter Emery
Burney, Charles: The Present State of Music in France and Italy
Burney, Charles: The Present State of Music in Germany, The Netherlands ...
Burney, Charles: An Account of the Musical Performances ... Handel
Burney, Karl: Nachricht von Georg Friedrich Handel's Lebensumstanden.
Burns, Robert (jnr): The Caledonian Musical Museum (1810 volume)
Cobbett, W.W.: Cobbett's Cyclopedic Survey of Chamber Music. (2 vols.)
Corrette, Michel: Le Maitre de Clavecin
Crimp, Bryan: Dear Mr. Rosenthal ... Dear Mr. Gaisberg ...
Crimp, Bryan: Solo: The Biography of Solomon
d'Indy, Vincent: Beethoven: Biographie Critique
d'Indy, Vincent: Beethoven: A Critical Biography
d'Indy, Vincent: César Franck (in French)
Fischhof, Joseph: Versuch einer Geschichte des Clavierbaues
Frescobaldi, Girolamo: D'Arie Musicali per Cantarsi. Primo Libro & Secondo Libro.
Geminiani, Francesco: The Art of Playing the Violin.
Handel; Purcell; Boyce; Green et al: Calliope or English Harmony: Volume First.
Hawkins, John: A General History of the Science and Practice of Music (5 vols.)
Herbert-Caesari, Edgar: The Science and Sensations of Vocal Tone
Herbert-Caesari, Edgar: Vocal Truth
Hopkins and Rimboult: The Organ. Its History and Construction.
Hunt, John: some 40 discographies – see list of discographies
Isaacs, Lewis: Hänsel and Gretel. A Guide to Humperdinck's Opera.
Isaacs, Lewis: Königskinder (Royal Children) A Guide to Humperdinck's Opera.
Lacassagne, M. l'Abbé Joseph : Traité Général des élémens du Chant.
Lascelles (née Catley), Anne: The Life of Miss Anne Catley.
Mainwaring, John: Memoirs of the Life of the Late George Frederic Handel
Malcolm, Alexander: A Treaty of Music: Speculative, Practical and Historical
Marx, Adolph Bernhard: Die Kunst des Gesanges, Theoretisch-Practisch
May, Florence: The Life of Brahms
Mellers, Wilfrid: Angels of the Night: Popular Female Singers of Our Time
Mellers, Wilfrid: Bach and the Dance of God

Travis & Emery Music Bookshop
17 Cecil Court, London, WC2N 4EZ, United Kingdom.
Tel. (+44) 20 7240 2129

Music and Books published by Travis & Emery Music Bookshop:

Mellers, Wilfrid: Beethoven and the Voice of God
Mellers, Wilfrid: Caliban Reborn - Renewal in Twentieth Century Music
Mellers, Wilfrid: François Couperin and the French Classical Tradition
Mellers, Wilfrid: Harmonious Meeting
Mellers, Wilfrid: Le Jardin Retrouvé, The Music of Frederic Mompou
Mellers, Wilfrid: Music and Society, England and the European Tradition
Mellers, Wilfrid: Music in a New Found Land: ... ... American Music
Mellers, Wilfrid: Romanticism and the Twentieth Century (from 1800)
Mellers, Wilfrid: The Masks of Orpheus: ...... the Story of European Music.
Mellers, Wilfrid: The Sonata Principle (from c. 1750)
Mellers, Wilfrid: Vaughan Williams and the Vision of Albion
Panchianio, Cattuffio: Rutzvanscad Il Giovine.
Pearce, Charles: Sims Reeves, Fifty Years of Music in England.
Pettitt, Stephen: Philharmonia Orchestra: Complete Discography 1945-1987
Playford, John: An Introduction to the Skill of Musick.
Purcell, Henry et al: Harmonia Sacra ... The First Book, (1726)
Purcell, Henry et al: Harmonia Sacra ... Book II (1726)
Quantz, Johann: Versuch einer Anweisung die Flöte traversiere zu spielen.
Rameau, Jean-Philippe: Code de Musique Pratique, ou Methodes.
Rastall, Richard: The Notation of Western Music.
Rimbault, Edward: The Pianoforte, Its Origins, Progress, and Construction.
Rousseau, Jean Jacques: Dictionnaire de Musique
Rubinstein, Anton: Guide to the proper use of the Pianoforte Pedals.
Sainsbury, John S.: Dictionary of Musicians. Vol. 1. (1825). 2 vols.
Simpson, Christopher: A Compendium of Practical Musick in Five Parts
Spohr, Louis: Autobiography
Spohr, Louis: Grand Violin School
Tans'ur, William: A New Musical Grammar; or The Harmonical Spectator
Terry, Charles Sanford: Four-Part Chorals of J.S. Bach. (German & English)
Terry, Charles Sanford: Joh. Seb. Bach, Cantata Texts, Sacred and Secular.
Terry, Charles Sanford: The Origins of the Family of Bach Musicians.
Tosi, Pierfrancesco: Opinioni de' Cantori Antichi, e Moderni
Van der Straeten, Edmund: History of the Violoncello, The Viol da Gamba ...
Van der Straeten, Edmund: History of the Violin, Its Ancestors... (2 vols.)
Walther, J. G.: Musicalisches Lexikon ober Musicalische Bibliothec (1732)

Travis & Emery Music Bookshop
17 Cecil Court, London, WC2N 4EZ, United Kingdom.
Tel. (+44) 20 7240 2129

© Travis & Emery 2009

www.ingramcontent.com/pod-product-compliance
Lightning Source LLC
Chambersburg PA
CBHW071837230426
43671CB00012B/1984